RESISTANCE
AND
RENEWAL

Surviving the Indian
Residential School

Celia Haig-Brown, M.A.

ARSENAL PULP PRESS
Vancouver

RESISTANCE AND RENEWAL
Copyright © 1988 Celia Haig-Brown &
The Secwepemc Cultural Education Society

Eighth printing: 2006

ARSENAL PULP PRESS
200 - 341 Water Street
Vancouver, BC
Canada V6B 1B8
arsenalpulp.com

The publisher gratefully acknowledges the support of the Canada Council for the Arts and the British Columbia Arts Council for its publishing program, and the Government of Canada through the Book Publishing Industry Development Program, and the Government of British Columbia through the Book Publishing Tax Credit Program, for its publishing activities.

Text design by the Vancouver Desktop Publishing Centre
Edited for the Press by Linda Field
Photos reproduced with the permission of the Kamloops Museum & Archives

Printed and bound in Canada

LIBRARY AND ARCHIVES CANADA CATALOGUING IN PUBLICATION

Haig-Brown, Celia, 1947-

Resistance and renewal : surviving the Indian residential school

Bibliography: p.
Includes index.
ISBN 0-88978-189-3

  1. Indians of North America — British Columbia — Education. 2. Indians of North America — Canada — Education. 3. Shuswap Indians — Education. 4. Kamloops Indian Residential School. 5. Residence and education. I. Title.
E96.5.H34 1987   371.97'97'0711   C88-091037-2

ISBN13 978-0-88978-189-4

*To all the people whose stories
are still untold.*

CONTENTS

PREFACE

The research for *Resistance and Renewal* was conducted between December 1985 and June 1986. For the First Nations people who attended them, residential schools have always been an issue. But back then, they weren't talking openly about what the schools meant to them. The stories often remained hidden in memories, either because they were too painful to articulate, or because of the belief that that was just the way things were.

Since 1986, many more stories have surfaced. Books such as those by the Ojibway Basil Johnston and Oblate Thomas Lascelles augment and complicate our understandings of Canadian residential schools. Conferences in Vancouver and Williams Lake in 1991 offered support to the many survivors of residential schools who sought a safe environment in which to present their experiences and call for government and church response. Courses for band planners and social service workers now include components which focus on the impact of residential schools on the people with whom they work. Many more books remain to be written, and many more stories remain to be told.

When I worked in the Kamloops area in preparation for this book, I hoped it would be more than an academic exercise. I wanted the time and energy First Nations people had offered me to be useful to others. If I learned my lessons well, perhaps I could put these stories in some form which would allow others to share their richhness and insight. People who were ignorant of this aspect of Canada's history might come to see what it meant for those who had experienced it.

Resistance and Renewal has had some success. It has been used in university courses from anthropology to education and history, and sells well at the Union of B.C. Indian Chiefs' bookstore in Vancouver. I meet and talk with First Nations people who have read it, and many acknowledge the similarities of their experiences, whether they attended school in Fraser Lake, the Kootenays, or Port Alberni. Some ask advice about documenting their specific experiences.

The book has, of course, been criticized, particularly by those

historians and sociologists who looked for a linear documenta-
tion of the students' development. They did not find it—though
I occasionally nodded in the direction of positivistic research.
They found instead an ethnography which focussed on the fact
that all the subjects shared the experience of attending the
Kamloops Indian Residential School, as well as the willingness
to talk about those experiences. And the people interviewed
share the common experience of being First Nations people in
Canada today. During the interviews, I recognized certain dominant perceptions and persistent attitudes, regardless of the
time of the students' attendance. Even those who remember the
school as being their only source of food and shelter were
devastated by the long-term effects of separation from family,
community, culture, and language.

  Resistance and Renewal has also been criticized by some First
Nations people who see my work as an unwanted intervention
in First Nations business. But it is important to remember that
the story of the schools is one in which non-Natives played a
central role. Some non-Natives said these stories are essential
for all people who want to know the history of Canada. The
Latin American Jewish feminist, Judith Moschkovich, says that
"it is not the duty of the oppressed to educate the oppressor."
People should find and read existing materials, she says, so that
when the opportunity arises, they can engage in informed
conversations with those whose voices have been too long
excluded from mainstream histories. I think of the strength and
commitment of the people with whom I spoke, those who gave
me pieces of their lives to put on paper for others to read.
Together we had hoped that we could contribute to a more
complete understanding—and ultimately to more equitable
treatment—of First Nations people.

  The structure of the book makes a clear distinction between
what the people said to me and my interpretations. That is
important for those who would search for other possibilities
within the words. On the other hand, I find the interpretation
I chose as appropriate and as useful now as I did then.

  Sexual abuse in residential schools has become a major focus
of court action and therapeutic work for survivors. It has also
become an endless source of stories for the media. People did
talk to me about abuse, usually after the tape recorder was
turned off. In respect for those who did not want their words

to be recorded, I included only some general statements about the abuse they mentioned. It is important to reiterate that sexual abuse is only one aspect of the assaults which the children in the schools endured. The stories we are inundated with by the mass media are coloured by sensationalism and a new-found attitude toward the prior silence of the victims. Regrettably, the sensationalism tends to isolate the abuse from a context in which First Nations' languages, spiritual beliefs, and entire cultural competencies were negated. First Nations people were expected to become like non-Natives—to serve as human resources for the developing industrial Canada.

Throughout these onslaughts described in the stories which follow, the people resisted and found strength within that resistance. Aspects of their family cultures persisted, enough to build on, enough to feed the renewal process which continues through constitutional restructuring, setbacks in land claims negotiations, and the myriad of other struggles between governments and First Nations people. The gains are signficant; there is no going back. Some of the determination First Nations people now exhibit found its roots in the resistance to the invasive culture of the schools designed to annihilate First Nations cultures.

I saw this strength in the Secwepemc people in the Kamloops area as they continued the process of taking control of their education. I knew the stories of the residential school and wondered how their current active commitment to transforming education arose from such oppressive circumstances. Some of the answers lie in the powerful commentaries found in this book. It is the power to resist and to maintain a sense of culture despite all odds which brings First Nations people to the cultural reaffirmation increasingly evident in Canada today.

—CELIA HAIG-BROWN,
October 1991

ACKNOWLEDGEMENTS

The author-quiltmaker thanks those members of the Shuswap, Thompson, Lillooet and Chilcotin Nations who shared so freely in allowing her to listen to the stories. Thanks are also due to the Secwepemc Cultural Education Society Board and staff, particularly Rita Jack and Robert Matthew for their guidance, suggestions and trust.

I am grateful to my brother Alan Haig-Brown for his support, to my advisor Dr. Jane Gaskell for her confidence and her discerning comments, and to the members of my committee, Jo-ann Archibald and Dr. Art More, for their most helpful suggestions. Thanks to Randy Fred, my publisher, for his patience and encouragement, and to my sister, Valerie Haig-Brown, and to Bill Maciejko, for their editorial comments. Special thanks to U.B.C.'s Ts'kel and Education Studies 479 students and Elaine Herbert for their critical discussion.

FOREWORD

The World Conference of Indigenous Peoples' Education, held in Vancouver in 1987, brought together Native people from six continents to discuss Native peoples' education around the world. Within such a diverse group a familiar and broad-ranging set of themes emerged. Of particular interest to me were the stories told by a group of Coorgs, a people indigenous to India, who reported on the state of the residential schools there.

It was a familiar story. I hadn't realized it was a world-wide story.

The similarities between modern life among the Coorgs and among North American Native people were eerie; alcoholism, suicide, lack of economic self-sufficiency, racism, dependency . . . and residential schools, to which the Coorgs are still forced to send their children.

They were strangers from halfway around the world, but they could have been Canadian Indians talking: victims in the long process of colonization. Colonization works the same way everywhere, its policies geared toward displacement and elimination of indigenous culture: genocide. The residential school, wherever it has appeared, has been part of that policy.

Colonizers utilize two forms of genocide: intentional and unintentional. The intentional forms include residential schools, land grabbing, and downright murder. Unintentional forms include the introduction of disease (although in some cases this was intentional), which has reduced the populations of the original inhabitants of the Americas more than has intentional forms of genocide.

The elimination of language has always been a primary stage in a process of cultural genocide. This was the primary function of the residential school. My father, who attended Alberni Indian Residential School for four years in the twenties, was physically tortured by his teachers for speaking Tseshaht: they pushed sewing needles through his tongue, a routine punishment for language offenders.

Today Native people are actively restoring and preserving their languages, although many have been lost forever. And Native people are taking more control of the education of their children. They have no choice. The colonial system has failed to educate Native children adequately. Statistics for Native achievement prove this. In a few communities a fascinating role-reversal is taking place whereby non-Indian students are attending Native-run schools and learning the local Native language. For children attaining a 'sense of place,' isn't this more reasonable than those non-Indian children learning French?

The needle tortures suffered by my father affected all my family. (I have six brothers and six sisters.) My Dad's attitude became "why teach my children Indian if they are going to be punished for speaking it?" so he would not allow my mother to speak Indian to us in his presence. I never learned how to speak my own language. I am now, therefore, truly a 'dumb Indian'.

Dodger's Cove, outside Bamfield on the west coast of Vancouver Island, was our paradise. The one-room shack was small but comfortable with a small generator for power, an outhouse out back, and a well for fresh water. We lived alone on the island. Across the cove an elder relative lived with his grandson, who was one year older than me. The cove was protected so well that, at the age of four, I was able to row a canoe across on my own to visit and play; it wasn't very far, but at my age and size it seemed like a long way.

At the far end of the fifty-yard beach there was a bed of clams and oysters. I remember going there with our dog, Nipper, to snack on raw clams. I would go outside the cove with my mother in our canoe at low tides gathering delicacies: sea urchins, black katy chitons, goose-neck barnacles, mussels; it makes my mouth water just thinking about it. My father would bring home fish, deer, ducks, and seals. This was my life before the residential school.

My father was a commercial troller. His boat, Gabriola Belle, was small by today's standards but it housed our family adequately on many occasions. Dodger's Cove was only a temporary residence. We lived on several of the small islands now known as the Broken Island Chain in Pacific Rim Park. The small generator allowed mobility as there were several vacant shacks in the area.

During the school year I was the oldest child. I knew my older brothers and sisters were in the residential school but it never occurred to me that I would also have to go there.

Summer months were different. With my older siblings at home I was no longer the oldest. Since we lost one brother and one sister who would have been between my next older brother and myself, our family seemed more like two separate families. As the number seven child I seemed to be the oldest of a second family; the group that didn't have to worry or think about going to school because our lives revolved around food gathering and playing on the beaches.

I remember being four years old when we made the four-hour boat journey to Port Alberni to return the older kids to school. I never felt sad for them. Quite the contrary, I felt glad they were returning to school, out of my hair. When my father was fishing, which was most of the time, I was the man of the house.

The next September, when I was five, we went to Port Alberni, as usual. The kids went with my parents in taxis to the school, as usual. When my parents returned we gathered up my younger brother and sister and climbed into a taxi. I had no idea where we were going; I assumed we were going to the reserve to visit my grandparents or aunt.

Prior to this I had only seen the residential school from the Somass River. Up close it looked massive, intimidating. Without any explanation they brought me in the front door where two staff members were waiting. My parents exchanged a few words with the staff then scooted out the front door. I took off as fast as I could after Mom and Dad. A pair of huge hands grabbed me and picked me up. I began screaming and kicking, calling for my parents. I watched the taxi depart. Everything was moving in slow motion; it was a nightmare, it couldn't be happening.

My family continued migrating within the Broken Island Chain and nearby Indian fishing villages until I was about ten or eleven years old, when my father built a house on the Tseshaht Reservation No. 2, in Port Alberni. This house was totally financed by my father, a rarity in those days because of the dependency on the Federal Government for housing. My father was very proud of this fact, and rightly so.

At Alberni the boys wore grey prison-style shirts, denim overall pants, grey work socks and heavy army-style boots. The boots were supposed to make it difficult for us to run away. We were each assigned a number, which had to be written on everything we wore. This had been the wardrobe for many years. When the Department of Indian Affairs took over the school, dress changed dramatically. It was like Christmas; striped polo shirts (a choice of three colours), regular blue denim jeans, lighter boots, and regular socks. Each year the dress became more varied.

Food in the school was rarely fit for swine, but the staff had their own cook and dining room and they ate like kings. To this day, I cannot eat macaroni & cheese, bologna, or scalloped potatoes, because of the way these were prepared in the school. The menus rarely changed, even after the federal government took over, and the kids were hungry most of the time. We used to sneak potatoes out of the storage room and bake them in the garbage incinerator. Sometimes guys would be able to sneak into the kitchen at night. I still envy them because I had night blindness and was never able to participate in those feasts. When I was first bussed into town to public schools the brown bag lunches we brought from the residential school were embarrassing: no dressing in the sandwiches, rotten fruit, nothing to drink.

Lack of adequate nourishment did, however, make us lean. The one real escape we had from the monotony of the school was sports. We were fortunate in having as one of our teachers a British coach. Alberni had a good gymnastics team and some of the best soccer, basketball, and softball teams around. I loved soccer and softball. My tunnel vision made basketball difficult for me to play. Two students from the school were offerred professional contracts with a British soccer team.

Religion was stuffed down our throats. We had to go to church every morning; on Sunday we had to go morning and night. The principal was the minister, providing the younger kids with many hours of astonishment as he sat on stage chewing his tongue, while we sat in the auditorium waiting for the service to begin and, better still, to end. It was always a fight to stay awake. The grade three teacher was the piano player. Her music was the only good thing about the services. She was amazingly proficient despite having lost her right hand and forearm to polio. If she could play despite a disability I was sure I could play; I loved the sound of the piano, but we were not allowed near it.

The student society was strongly hierarchical; powerful students became leaders of clusters of students, in a process similar to socialization inside Oakalla Prison. In fact many people I know who have been to Oakalla Prison tell me that doing hard time was easier than doing time in Alberni.

During my early days at Alberni the big thing for displaying rank was sock-washing. In the main building there were five dormitories for the boys and five for the girls. High school students stayed in Edward Peake Hall. In total, about three hundred students attended AIRS each year. The boys in the main building, aged five to sixteen or so, had to wash their own socks every night. But the tough and the powerful never washed their own socks. Retribution was cruel if you refused to wash a tough guy's socks. But alliances were built amongst tribal groups and relatives: "No way, man, I don't have to wash your damn socks, my bigger brother will beat you up." Of course, the older brother had to be bigger and tougher, and also had to be bigger and tougher than the aggressor's superior or protector, if he was fortunate enough to have one.

One of my cousins recalls that time in these words: "Man, we were so tough and cool in the residential school, ten Fonzies couldn't stand up to one of us." Yep, tough and cool, the essence of survival.

Alliances didn't always follow the pattern of tribal affiliations or family. One of my worst (and most embarrassing) recollections involved one of my brothers, who for some reason didn't like me. He had two go-fers, sock-washers, who were brothers. I got into a fight with them. I was so upset, my adrenalin was flowing so rapidly, I almost beat both of them up. My brother, instead of standing up for me, stood up for his go-fers.

Confused and angry, with my brother and his two go-fers chasing me, I ran into the playing field next to the school. I was crying; this angered me even more because it was uncool to cry. Running away from violence was also uncool. What a mess. A crowd began to gather to watch the action. Making my situation worse I began picking up rocks to throw at the three, the ultimate in being uncool. Throwing rocks was considered sissy, we were expected to take our licks. The scene—a crowd of guys watching us, the two brothers trying to approach me so they could beat the shit out of me, me throwing rocks—still to this day haunts me and gives me nightmares. I have many nightmares about the school.

This breakdown in my relationship with my brother (which is now okay) bothered me for years. But the worst that happened to me in the way of family relationships involves my father. We were allowed to go home two months during the summer. My father, after settling in Port Alberni, had to carry ice and go on ten-day trolling trips. I rarely saw him during the summer. His type of fishing was hard work. When he was home in the summer it was not always pleasant. Naturally, I grew up not knowing much about my father. Having so many brothers and sisters made it more difficult to spend time with him. I don't remember ever having a heart-to-heart conversation with him until after he retired.

I did get to go out on a couple of his ten-day trips. God, I hated it: out on the ocean for ten days, rough seas, seasickness, the awful smell of the exhaust and bilge, gloominess, the long days, a skipper (my father) who expected me to know everything about trolling. Whenever I made a mistake he would say, "What the hell do they teach you in that school anyway?" These experiences pushed my father and me further apart. My great hatred of the residential school springs from this: it took away the opportunity for me to grow up with my father. I never did get close to him until only a few years before he passed away.

The institutional environment did nothing to prepare students for assimilation. Most students were ignorant about survival. There was no opportunity to learn simple everyday tasks like cooking or any kind of maintenance. This made integration difficult. In high school I felt out of place when cars were the topic of discussion because I didn't know a thing about car engines.

Integration was a tough thing to handle. I was in grade seven when they started bussing us into the public schools in town. Immediately we were labelled as Indians, but we had a second label because we were being bussed in from the residential school: a lower class of Indian. The shock was too much for me; my grades dropped, my sense of self-worth disappeared, learning became a chore.

One of my cousins reflected that his separation after eighteen years of marriage was probably due to his inability to express emotions. Without parental love and without parental role models students were not adequately equipped to fit into the mainstream society. My cousin said, "It was important not to cry or show emotion when being strapped by old Caldwell; no matter how pissed off he got or how hard he strapped you, you could not cry." Caldwell was the principal when I first attended the school. He performed most of the punishment for the boys in the school; ironically, he also did all the preaching.

I was appalled, when first meeting with Celia to discuss publishing this book, to learn that some people who had read the manuscript believed some of it not to be true; the nuns *couldn't* have been that mean to those children. Well, the nuns at the Kamloops Indian Residential School could indeed be that mean, as the supervisors, administrators and teachers at practically all Indian boarding schools could be.

One of my older sisters recalls the strap Mrs. Rothwell used on the girls as being one-half inch thick, three inches wide, and about three feet long. She had seen the dreaded weapon close-up. She remembers girls being strapped most frequently for sneaking off the school grounds. This was a favourite pastime and preoccupation—busting out of the hellhole. Many dangerous risks were taken, such as climbing through the window, down three stories on a rope of bed sheets tied together.

Most of the boys' supervisors were sadists, consisting mainly of men kicked out of the RCMP or retired from the armed forces. Their jobs had to be the bottom of the work force barrel at the time. One supervisor used to stand us in line for hours at a time and amuse himself with sadistic acts. This guy eventually committed suicide in a Vancouver hotel room.

I was first sexually abused by a student when I was six years old, and by a supervisor, an ex-Navy homosexual, when I was eight. Homosexuality was prevalent in the school. I learned how to use sexuality to my advantage, as did many other students. Sexual favours brought me protection, sweets (a rarity in the school), and even money to buy booze. But this had its long-term effects . . . including alcoholism, the inability to touch people, and an 'I don't care' attitude.

Learning about sexuality in an institutional environment creates confusion and aberration. The boys and girls were not permitted to associate with each other except at infrequent dances; the genders were even separated in the classroom.

Nevertheless, there was always a way to have sex. One of the supervisors at Alberni during the fifties was easily bribed to open the door to the infirmary on the second floor which separated the boys from the girls. All it took was a bottle of whiskey and he'd open the door and then go back to bed and ignore the stampede to the girls' side. Mrs. Rothwell, the girls' head supervisor, slept like a log. As soon as her snoring stopped all the humping stopped; what a way to make love—in a dormitory of squeaky beds, listening to Rothwell snoring. This was a little before my time, of course. When the boys' supervisor was replaced it was back to encounters behind one of the school buildings—very uncomfortable. During my time the kids were allowed outside the school boundaries for a short time Sunday afternoon, a great opportunity to get it on.

I believe the reason so little attention has been paid to Indian residential schools in North America is that the churches were connected to so many of them. Native people, being a spiritual race, have always been reluctant to criticize any kind of church. Recent court cases charging priests, former supervisors of residential schools, with sexual abuse indicate Native people are willing to deal with the pain and the shame in order to work towards healing those who found residential schools to be a negative experience.

The Department of Indian Affairs was responsible for social services. After my parents relocated to Port Alberni from the west coast one of my aunts was unable to care for her children so my mother took three of her sons, my first cousins, in to board with the family. I didn't understand the reason for this at my young age; all I could see was that my parents were continuing to send me off to the residential school, only 200 yards away, and my cousins were living at my parents' house. This situation alienated me further from my father. I realize now that this had nothing to do with any lack of love from my parents. They made their decisions based on economics and options available to them at the time. If the entire family, including the cousins, lived in the small four-bedroom house there would have been eighteen of us crammed in. In fact, one summer there were actually twenty-one of us living in that tiny house.

This crowded environment made studying difficult. I took advantage of the 'boarding-out program' for my grade twelve. I had always been at the top of the class grades one through six;

grade seven was my first year at a white school and my grades dropped to a 'C' average. My grades picked up a bit until grade ten, my first year going to school from home. I barely squeaked by grade eleven. I realized the only way I would graduate would be to board out, so I took my grade twelve in Nanaimo and managed to pass with fairly good marks.

It was easy for me to leave Port Alberni. I never did have a feeling of permanence there because the further I could get away from the residential school, the better.

The staff made it clear to us that we were not allowed to associate with the reservation kids, my own relatives. This made life uncomfortable for me during the summer months when I lived on the reservation. There was a wire fence encircling the school grounds. We were not allowed within ten feet of the fence. I was locked in in the winter and locked out in the summer. Understandably, I was not popular on the reserve, being a residential school kid. For friendship I turned to people who had moved to Port Alberni from the west coast of Vancouver Island, many of whom had attended the boarding school. This alienation was not the case with all my brothers and sisters who attended Alberni, though. Some fit into reservation life very well.

At the age of twelve booze discovered me. A beautiful escape from hell. The same year I experimented with drugs and began chainsmoking cigarettes. By the time I was fifteen booze was a real problem, and continued to be until only recently. I know this was the case with many people who attended residential schools. Booze was an easy escape.

I used booze to get kicked out of the school at the end of grade nine. One of my best buddies and I rustled up the cash. The building that had been used for grades one to three had been converted to dormitories after the big integration push. Boys and girls were housed in the building. The basement had a room that was used for dances. It had a movable panel separating the boys' side from the girls' side. During a dance one Saturday night, my buddy and I got nearly every girl in that dormitory drunk. It worked—my buddy and I were expelled— FREEDOM!

I look on my road to recovery from alcoholism as a process of de-assholification. No doubt the school messed up my head a lot, made a big asshole out of me. My point of reference for 'big' is the fact that I attempted suicide twice after I left the

school, another reason for seeing myself as a failure, both for
failing to do it and for wanting to do it.

But Indian people are durable people. We have survived
incredible onslaughts—residential schools being only one factor.
These days we are witnessing the revival of many traditions and
values, including teaching styles. Native people are being encouraged to get in touch with their culture and to use it for the
betterment of the people. Taking control of Indian education
is an important step.

Indian curriculum was introduced into the public school
system primarily to improve the academic achievement of Indian students and in this respect it failed. This does not mean,
however, that the concept of Indian curriculum is useless; in
fact, the trend should be towards more Indian curriculum in the
public school system. And now, especially after the World
Conference for Indigenous Peoples' Education, the thrust
should be, "Education into Culture, not Culture into Education." The closure of the residential schools makes this concept
more feasible because they were an obstacle for Native people
taking charge of their own destiny.

The resistance which Celia Haig-Brown examined took place
in the United States, as well as Canada. In the U.S. by 1899, there
were 148 Indian boarding schools and 225 Indian day schools,
with attendance of about 20,000 students. By 1950, attendance
was still only about 27,000 although the population had dou-
bled, indicating a strong resistance by the Native community.
In 1966, attendance was up to 140,000. Major J.S. Pratt was
responsible for the establishment of boarding schools in the
U.S. The objective was total integration and elimination of all
Indian cultures, like the Canadian objective.

The contents of *Resistance and Renewal* will be a useful tool
for the 'renewal' process for Native people; in understanding
the past, both Natives and others can live better lives in the
present and plan sensibly for the future.

—RANDY FRED
NEW WORLD MEDIA SOCIETY

INTRODUCTION

Few extensive studies of residential schools in British Columbia exist. Much of the extant literature dealing with Native education is based on materials written by Euro-Canadians with only minimal involvement of the people of whom they write. The few materials available which discuss residential schools usually present information from the perspective of the government or the missionaries whose policies controlled them. The purpose of this book is primarily to present Native perspectives of the Kamloops Indian Residential School, and to provide a limited overview of how Native education has evolved.

Thirteen interviews with Native people of the central Interior of British Columbia, former students of the school, form the nucleus of the study. Because the interior people traditionally have oral cultures, interviewing was deemed the most appropriate research technique. Through the study participants' own words, the experiences of leaving home, of arriving at school, of surviving the daily routines of the school, of resisting the oppressive structure imposed and, finally, of returning home, are restructured. Two main concepts, cultural invasion and resistance, are of paramount importance.

Participants were selected to represent various time periods of the school's operation. A conscious effort was made to maintain a balance between male and female views, positive and negative views and the views of students who attended for longer and shorter time spans. In addition, representatives from a number of different Shuswap bands and from bands outside the Shuswap Nation were selected. Efforts were also made to ensure Native participation in data analysis and interpretation. Background information on the three groups involved with the school—the Shuswap, the missionaries and the governments—was obtained from various archives and libraries.

The most outstanding feature which is revealed by this study is the extent and complexity of the resistance movement which the students and their families developed against the invasive presence of the residential school. The struggles for power and control within the school may be seen as a microcosm of the ongoing struggle of Native people with the Euro-Canadian presence in this country.

The need to develop a model different from the hierarchical one which church, state and academics too frequently have attempted to impose upon Native people—one based on authentic dialogue—is shown. Implications for further research, particularly of a qualitative nature, are numerous—from specific aspects of culture such as arranged marriages and language retention, to more general comparisons of the Kamloops Indian Residential School with other residential schools, and to more contemporary Native education, many possibilities are raised. Ultimately, what emerges is a picture of strong individuals and a strong culture growing, adapting and surviving.

CHAPTER 1
SETTING THE SCENE

"Three things stand out in my mind from my years at school: hunger; speaking English; and being called a heathen because of my grandfather."
George Manuel (1974: 63)

The Secwepemc, also known as Shuswap, were traditionally a migratory hunting, fishing, and gathering people *(Dawson, 1891; Teit, 1909)*. The people were migratory in that they travelled seasonally to traditional food gathering places. (See *Appendix E.*) Because of the severe winter climate of the surrounding Kamloops region, much of the summer was devoted to food gathering and preservation. In the late summer months, people travelled to and camped at salmon fishing grounds to catch and dry fish. Throughout the growing season, they gathered berries and roots from appropriate places and dried or used them in the preparation of food and utensils such as baskets. Hunting, a most important activity, was carried on through most of the year and often involved travel over great distance. Within the Secwepemc society existed all the complexities of culture: government, religion, science, technology, acknowledgement and celebration of life passages, traditions, and oral history, which included a theory of origin. As with all cultures, language served as an expression of and for the transmission of the culture.

Into the lives of this relatively stable and thriving culture came the white European. Initially the encounters were limited to exchanges with an itinerant fur trader who had little effect on the lifestyle of the people who met him. Trade goods which enhanced or made easier the work of the Native person were desirable. As European markets became more demanding and the West became more familiar, the North West Company began its push to establish trading posts to centralize efforts and reduce the travelling of employees *(Fisher, 1977)*. In 1812, close to the site of a winter village of Secwepemc, Fort Thompson was

27

founded at the confluence of two rivers known to the Europeans as the North and South Thompson.

About the same time, the Oblates of Mary Immaculate were intensifying their presence in British Columbia, following a somewhat disappointing time in what is now Washington state. Lack of support by the American government dampened the enthusiasm of those in control, and B.C. became the target of a new missionary thrust toward Indian people *(Cronin, 1960: 46)*. Sixty years after the founding of Fort Thompson, St. Louis Mission became a centre of operation under the auspices of Father Grandidier, O.M.I.

During their involvement in the Pacific Northwest, the Oblates had become acquainted with and, on many occasions, immersed in the lives of the Native people. Because of the limited numbers of priests and brothers working, one can assume that, in order to minister more effectively, the Oblates viewed settlement into an agrarian lifestyle as a positive step for Native people. Indeed, in their moves to 'Christianize and civilize' the Native people, the Oblates viewed the acquisition of farming skills as progress—one in line with white European standards. The migrant lifestyle of the Native people, because it was different from the European lifestyle, was seen as inherently wrong.

The introduction of Catholicism to the Secwepemc was a relatively easy process largely because of similarities between Secwepemc religious beliefs and those of the Catholics. While far from precise parallels, spirits similar to God the Father and Christ, his Son were recognized.

> The Shuswap believed in two great spirits they called the Old-One and Coyote. The Old-One . . . was all powerful . . . . The Old-One had as his chief assistant . . . a spirit called Coyote. Although the description of Coyote varies somewhat from the Christian idea of Jesus . . . there were enough similarities between the two figures to ensure familiarity for the Indians. Coyote was sent by the Old-One to travel over the world and put it to rights. (WHITEHEAD, 1981: 29-30)

Other similarities included the celebration of two annual festivals—Christmas or mid-winter and Easter or mid-summer— and the acknowledgement of individual guardian spirits.

Initially, the missionaries passed through the Secwepemc

territory preaching and converting. Shortly after B.C.'s entry
into Confederation in 1871 and the establishment of the St.
Louis Mission school for girls in 1878 *(Morse, 1949: 3)*, the
desirability of setting up an industrial school was crystallized.
As a continuation of the policy direction established by the Acts
of 1868 and 1869, the federal government saw the schools as
essential to educating the Indian to an agrarian lifestyle and
ultimately to assimilation into a 'superior', European society.
The Oblates recognized the advantages of working with children in isolation from the influence of their parents and of the
importance of daily religious participation and instruction in
molding young minds. It was these two forces—government and
church—which had the strongest cultural impact on the Native
people of the Kamloops area.

THE GOVERNMENTS

The Province of Canada in 1847 published a report based on
the ideas of Egerton Ryerson which formed the basis for future
directions in policy for Indian education and which, with Confederation, strongly influenced the development of schooling
for Native people in British Columbia *(Prentice and Houston,
1975: 218)*. Clearly expressed is the perception of superiority of
the European culture, the need " . . . to raise them [the Indians]
to the level of the whites," and the ever-increasing pressure to
take control of land out of Indian hands. At the same time the
contradictory need to isolate Indians from the evil influences
of white society is acknowledged. The general recommendations of the report were that Indians remain under the control
of the Crown rather than the provincial authority, that efforts
to Christianize the Indians and settle them in communities be
continued, and finally that schools, preferably manual labour
ones, be established under the guidance of missionaries *(Prentice and Houston: 220)*. Cultural oppression was becoming written policy. Within the discussion of the recommendations is the
following comment:

> Their education must consist not merely of the training of the
> mind, but of a weaning from the habits and feelings of their
> ancestors, and the acquirements of the language, arts and customs
> of civilized life. (PRENTICE AND HOUSTON: 220)

What clearer statement of an effort to destroy a culture could exist? The necessity of minimizing parental influence, another tool of cultural destruction, is further developed by Rev. Peter Jones, a Native convert to Christianity, in the same report:

> It is a notorious fact, that the parents in general exercise little or no control over their children, allowing them to do as they please. Being thus left to follow their own wills, they too frequently wander about the woods with their bows and arrows, or accompany their parents in their hunting excursions. (PRENTICE AND HOUSTON: 221)

The activities described were one of the main forms of traditional education for Native people: children learned by observing and following their parents and by doing the tasks expected of adults.

Following the establishment of the Indian Act of 1876, a consolidation of existing legislation, the government commissioned N.F. Davin to report on industrial schools established for Native people in the United States. Out of his report came the strong recommendations which resulted in the establishment of many residential schools across Canada, including the one at Kamloops, British Columbia. In the introduction to the report, Davin made references to President Grant's policy on the Indian question:

> The industrial school is the principal feature of the policy known as 'aggressive civilization.' (DAVIN, 1879: 1)

Other comments show that some of Davin's attitudes were reinforced by politicians involved with schools for Native people in the U.S. One point which frequently arose in discussions of Native education was that working with adults or children in day schools was ineffective.

> The experience of the United States is the same as our own as far as the adult Indian is concerned. Little can be done with him . . . . The child, again, who goes to a day school learns little, and what he learns is soon forgotten, while his tastes are fashioned at home, and his inherited aversion to toil is in no way combatted. (DAVIN: 2)

While positively endorsing the notion of residential schools for Indians in Canada, Davin's final comment is " . . . if anything is to be done with the Indian, we must catch him very young *(12)*.

Several amendments to the Indian Act of 1876 occurred before the implementation of Davin's recommendations. One amendment regarding schools in 1880 is significant in that it typifies government's contradictory approach to input from bands. Even something as straightforward as the teacher's denomination is not left to chance. "Chiefs could henceforth frame laws in the following areas:

> 1. As to what denomination the teacher of the school established on the reserve shall belong to; provided always, that he shall be of the same denomination as the majority of the band; and provided that the Catholic or Protestant minority likewise have a separate school with the approval of and under regulations to be made by the Governor in Council." (MILLER *ET AL*, 1978: 78)

What appears, at first glance, to give some autonomy to the Chief actually contains such confining conditions that the choice is already made.

In 1887, L. VanKoughnet, then Deputy Superintendent General of Indian Affairs, again stressed the need for schools for Native children. He wrote to the Right Honourable John A. Macdonald:

> That the country owes to the poor Indian to give him all that will afford him an equal chance of success in life with his white brother, by whom he has been supplanted (to use no stronger expression) in his possessions, goes without saying, and the gift for which we pray on his behalf, with a view to the discharge of this just debt, is the education of his children in such a way as will put beyond question their success in after life. (VAN KOUGHNET, 1887: 1)

This report recommended the establishment of day schools. By 1920 amendments to the Indian Act included compulsory school attendance of Indian children and industrial or boarding schools for Indians *(Miller, 1978: 115)*. Following these amendments were other minor ones relating to education. It is interesting to note that in 1920 in the House of Commons discussion of changes to the Indian Act, Deputy Superintendent General Duncan Campbell Scott stated clearly the idea that Indian cultures as such were to be eliminated.

> . . . Our object is to continue until there is not a single Indian in Canada that has not been absorbed into the body politic and there

is no Indian question, and no Indian department, that is the whole object of this Bill. (MILLER: 114)

Not until 1946 was there serious possibility for change in this attitude and in the expressed intent of Department of Indian Affairs policy. J. Allison Glen, Minister of Mines and Resources, declared: "The Indian, . . . should retain and develop many of his Native Characteristics, and . . . ultimately assume the full rights and responsibilities of democratic citizenship" *(Miller: 130)*. Also in 1946 discussions began for complete revamping of the Indian Act. For the first time, and only after initial strong resistance by committee members, Native input was actually permitted. Andrew Paull, President of the North American Indian Brotherhood, appeared before the Special Joint Committee. He was highly critical of the committee's lack of Indian representation. He condemned the existing Act as "an imposition, the carrying out of the most bureaucratic and autocratic system that was ever imposed upon any people in this world of ours" *(Special Joint Committee, 1947: 247)*. He spoke strongly for Indian self- government, and finally he commented that what was needed was:

> . . . to lift up the morale of the Indians in Canada. That is your first duty. There is no use in passing legislation about this or that if you do not lift up the morale of the people. The only way you can lift up the morale of any people is to let the members look after themselves and look after their people. (427)

His words fell upon deaf ears.

In 1947, anthropologist Diamond Jenness told the Committee what it wanted to hear. His "Plan for Liquidating Canada's Indian Problems within 25 Years" *(310-11)* recommended the abolition of Indian reserves and the establishment of an integrated educational system as the basis for assimilation. The never-ceasing attempt by the now dominant majority society to make the Indian disappear continued unabashed through this revision of the Indian Act. "The new Indian Act did not differ in many respects from previous legislation" *(Miller: 149)*. It did, however, serve as the beginning of the end for many residential schools because it allowed for Indian attendance in the public school system.

MISSIONARIES

George Manuel, the Secwepemc leader and author writes, "All areas of our lives which were not occupied by the Indian agent were governed by the priest" *(Manuel, 1974: 63)*. Such was the case with the residential school. While the government espoused assimilation of the Indian through Christianization and civilization, it turned the doing of the task over to the religious orders—priests and teachers.

The Oblates of Mary Immaculate was founded in 1812 by Eugene de Mazenod in France. He sought to improve the quality of priests and of religious instruction while asking members of the order to emphasize self-spiritual regeneration, strict observation of the rules of the order and, secondarily, preaching to the poor. Original involvement with North America came in response to a request from the bishop of Montreal. From there, a small group of Oblates moved west, arriving in Oregon in 1847. Here, the philosophies which were to guide much of the Oblate missionary work in British Columbia were put into action. In his "Instructions on Foreign Missions" de Mazenod had written:

> Every means should therefore be taken to bring the nomad tribes to abandon their wandering life and to build houses, cultivate fields and practise the elementary crafts of civilized life. (WHITE-HEAD: 118)

Second only to insisting that the Native people abandon their own religious beliefs and take up Christianity was the push for them to abandon their migratory lifestyle. From a practical point of view, it proved very difficult to minister to people who were frequently on the move.

Fort Kamloops, a North West Company trading post founded in 1812 and, since time immemorial, an important site of winter homes for the Secwepemc, was a logical site for the establishment of a mission. Father Demers, an Oblate, was the first missionary to visit the Kamloops area in 1842. In 1878, Father Grandidier was appointed rector and bursar of the permanent St. Louis Mission. The original church and mission were located two and a half miles west of the present city centre. Father LeJacq served as supervisor from 1880-1882 and was succeeded by Father LeJeune in 1883. Although the Oblates previously had been operating a school for the children in a different location, in 1893 they took control of the permanent residential school. Father A.M. Carion served as the director of the school and, with some time away, remained in charge until 1916. While the priests were frequently busy travelling to preach to the Native bands of the area, their policies served to control the direction of the school. Father Carion, in a report from Kamloops Indian Residential School, states:

> We keep constantly before the mind of the pupils the object which the government has in view. . .which is to civilize the Indians and to make them good, useful and law-abiding members of society. A continuous supervision is exercised over them, and no infraction of the rules of morality and good manners is left without due correction. (CRONIN, 1960: 215)

The prime objectives of the Oblates were to control the lives of the Native people spiritually and in terms of lifestyle. Although their impact on Native people was very different from the whiskey trade and profit-seeking exploitation of some Europeans, it was exploitation in that the Oblates created a growing need for themselves in the Native people's lives. Because the missionaries had more extensive knowledge of Jesus Christ than Native people, once converted, they had to rely on this source of spirituality. Only priests could say Mass and offer the sacraments essential to the practising Catholic.

In British Columbia, the missionaries and governments worked hand in hand to deal with the Indian 'problem'. Government must have seen the religious order's efforts to control as most beneficial. Rather than sending soldiers and guns to control the lives of the owners of the land, the governments had the missionaries who influenced the Native people to limit their movements, take up an agrarian lifestyle, and abandon their culture.

The Oblates noticed that they were much more effective with Native people who had not been involved with the corruptive influences of some white traders. In 1861, Father Chirouse wrote:

> . . . I find it much more difficult to reclaim and teach those who are brought much in contact with the evil-disposed and immoral among the whites than is the case with those who are differently situated. (CRONIN: 139)

This recognition led to an even stronger push for control of Native people's lives. It was seen as an advantage to separate the Native people from the white settlements and, in the beginning, even from the English language. In a letter to Father LeJeune in 1892, L.N. Saintonge states:

> I agree with you that to teach English to the Indian is too much of a task. Besides they always learn it too soon for their own good. Unfortunately, when the Indians come to know English, they are more disposed to have relations with the whites, and you know what the result is of their intercourse. No, no, teach them no English. Let them learn it how they may, and as late as possible.

Although his words suggest that acquisition of English is inevitable, one can assume that he hopes to have Christianity ingrained before exposure to evil influences.

Despite its good intentions, this desire for control over Native people partially through segregation and more directly through the destruction of their traditional lifestyle reveals the invasive nature of the Oblates' work. References to 'my Indians' are frequent and this possessiveness, while showing attachment to the people, also belittles and relegates the people to being possessions of another human being. Paulo Freire, in his discussion of cultural invasion, refers to well-intentioned professionals who invade not as a deliberate ideology but as an expression of their upbringing (1970: 154). He goes on to point out that cultural invasion "always involves a parochial view of reality, a static perception of the world and the imposition of this world view upon another" (159). Robin Fisher summarizes missionary efforts as follows:

> Because the missionaries did not separate Western Christianity and Western civilization, they approached Indian culture as a whole and demanded a total transformation of the Indian proselyte. Their aim was the complete destruction of the traditional integrated Indian way of life. The missionaries demanded even more far-reaching transformation than the settlers and they pushed it more aggressively than any other group of whites. (1977: 144-45)

Education was seen as a primary tool in effecting this transformation. In a vein similar to the government's notion of 'getting them while they are young', the Oblates saw tremendous possibilities in the establishment of residential schools. Here the students could be isolated from the cultural influences of their parents and a daily, systematic inculcation of Christian theory and practice became possible. Attempts to control became close to absolute in that students were expected to attend from August to June and visits from home were strictly limited. In a reversal of Saintonge's recommendation, the use of English became mandatory. Through efforts to prohibit the Native languages, the very base of culture was attacked.

In Kamloops, the permanent residential school was built on land purchased by the government at the edge of what is now, the Kamloops Indian Reserve. It was across the river from the town, providing the separation deemed optimal. In addition, it was several miles from the Indian village itself. The government had refused to purchase the buildings owned by the Oblates some miles away because it was felt that they were asking too much money. In 1890, three two-storey wooden buildings were completed at the present site and provided separate dormitories for boys and girls, a living area for teachers, classrooms, and a play area.

After a faltering start under the guidance of lay teacher Michael Hagan, the school was taken over by the Oblates in 1893. The Sisters of St. Ann also played a major role in working with the girls. Sister Mary Joachim started at the school in 1890, left shortly after, but returned in 1894 when the Oblates had taken over and remained until her death in 1907 (Kamloops Souvenir Edition, 1977: 8). In 1923, the new brick building was completed to replace the one destroyed by fire. Throughout most of its operation until its closure in 1966, the K.I.R.S. was guided by the Oblates assisted by the Sisters of St. Ann. In the usual male-female hierarchy within the Church, the Oblate priests controlled policy and served as administrators while the Sisters were expected to work obediently as teachers, child care workers, and supervisors along with the Oblate brothers, the laborers of the order.

Most students who attended the school fell within the governmental jurisdiction called the Kamloops Agency. This area included the southern Shuswap Bands of Bonaparte, ChuChua, Skeetchestn, Kamloops, Adams Lake, Chase, Neskonlith (see Appendix E), and several bands of Thompson Indians of the Nicola Valley. People from the Nicola Valley could choose to send children to St. Joseph's School in Lytton if they were Protestant and to St. Louis Mission in Kamloops if they were Catholic. In addition, some children from the Chilcotin and coastal bands attended the school. Following the 1916 Mc-Kenna-McBride Commission hearings, day schools were built on several reserves located some distance from Kamloops. Rising birth rates and enforced attendance after 1920 provided students not only for these schools but also an increasing number for the residential school.

THE SECWEPEMC

The Secwepemc whose children enrolled at that first residential school in 1893 had little experience with the formal European style of schooling offered by the Oblates. They saw childhood and schooling as an inseparable part of the on-going process of life and living.

> The methods used to teach skills for everyday living and to instill values and principles were participation and example. Within communities, skills were taught by every member, with Elders playing a very important role. Education for the child began at the time he or she was born. The child was prepared for his role in life whether it be hunter, fisherman, wife, or mother. This meant that each child grew up knowing his place in the system . . . . Integral to the traditional education system was the participation of the family and community as educators. (JACK, 1985: 9)

While warning of the danger of generalizing, Mary Ashworth (1979) says of traditional education amongst the diverse tribal groups in British Columbia:

> Education was the responsibility of all and it was a continuous process. Parents, grandparents and other relatives naturally played a major role, but other members of the tribe particularly the elders helped to shape the young people. (6)

In the early part of this century, James Teit, an ethnographer who learned the Shuswap language and spent his life working with Native people of the Central Interior of British Columbia, wrote extensively of the Shuswap people's traditional lifestyle. Children had few responsibilities or duties until they reached puberty. Although he does not comment in detail on Shuswap childhood, Teit points out that children of the Thompson, a closely related tribe to the South, had few restrictions. They had to rise early, wash frequently in cold water and limit their play after sunset. Shuswap children also participated in a complex ceremony twice a year called 'whipping the children' in which they were encouraged to overcome fear and ultimately demonstrate courage *(Teit, 1900: 308-309)*. Other than that, puberty was the time of focus on training. Girls were assisted by a grandmother, mother or aunt and spent a year in isolation practising all the work which a woman must do. Boys, isolating themselves for shorter periods of time, followed a similar pattern when their voices changed or they dreamed of women, arrows and canoes, but their training could last several years *(Teit, 1909: 587-90)*. In addition to this specialized training, in the evenings elders spent much time telling stories which emphasized ethical concepts and myths important to the people. Frequently time was spent addressing the young people directly.

> These were the times when the old people would address the young, and then they would admonish them to follow the rules of proper ethical conduct. (617)

The startling differences between Shuswap education and that of the residential school are numerous. Education with the Shuswap was a responsibility shared by family and community. Only at puberty did children remove themselves from the community for any length of time. Generally education was on-going, not focussed specifically on young people. The myths and stories told by the elders were directed not only at children but were a part of the life-blood of the community. With the residential school, children were removed from their community, placed in large groups and expected to follow a tight schedule. The adults with whom they had contact had very definite ideas about the children's need for changes in language, beliefs and lifestyle. The oppressive nature of the residential, religious schooling becomes clear.

CHAPTER 2
FROM HOME TO SCHOOL

"There was a lot more to our traditional education than just some 'Mickey Mouse' courses in moccasin making."
Nishga elder (Merkel, n.d.: n.p.)

AT HOME

The Shuswap children who attended Kamloops Indian Residential School had, before they reached school age, exposure to many aspects of traditional family life. As with all children, these initial experiences had tremendous impact on their eventual feelings about the residential school and its long term effects. In order to begin to understand these varying effects, one may examine the memories of the life and the culture of the children before they reached school.

The thing that I can remember about that little sod roof—it was like heaven to me I guess, 'cause it was so full of love and happiness, freedom. We'd help my grandma pack her wood and then she'd cook us something to eat. Then in the evening, she very seldom put a light in there because we didn't need a light . . . . At one end of that little sod roof . . . they pegged some little sticks or posts across, just so high and they put boards. And they filled it with that slough hay, full of that mint grass and that bed used to smell so nice. She would put a tarp over it and then quilts and that's where we all slept.

And my grandma would sit down, she had so much patience, I guess because she loved us so much . . . . She had a habit of always massaging our heads . . . she'd rub our backs. And she would start telling us little legends . . . . Sometimes we would hear the same legend over and over but I guess the lessons in those legends is what she was trying to get across to us . . . . At the end of the story, she would say 'Tat a maa' which meant 'See that man': this is what would happen if you don't do it or you do it.

To me when I look back, I can see me, especially in the spring when the little birds come back and you can hear them—makes you feel so good and I could just see me running around trying to catch a butterfly. And we never had bought shoes, we always had moccasins all the time. And I guess those were the nicest most beautiful times of my whole life . . . that freedom, my life so full of love. (SOPHIE: 6)

Within these words of remembrance lie several life values of great importance to Native people: the extended family exemplified by the grandmother and her teaching through legends, familial patience and love, the associations with the natural—mint grass, butterflies and freedom—and the contributions of even the littlest child to the work of the household. Life before residential school was seen as a positive, carefree time by most of the people interviewed. It was a time of learning small and larger tasks such as cooking, splitting and packing wood, falling trees, or mowing hay.

First of all, I sensed there was an expectation for me to do those [things] and because of that I started watching . . . . I learned how to chop wood after observing my father, my grandfather and my mother chopping wood and how safety conscious they were in taking care of the axe and making sure that no harm will be done. I would try on little pieces of wood, maybe the kindling and, if they did notice me holding the axe the wrong way, then they would point out the right way to do it.

We followed Dad while he worked on the farm mowing hay . . . . [In] playing, we also knew why he stopped the machine—it was plugged up—and what he did to clear it. He didn't use his hands; he used a stick to clear away in case the horses moved . . . . We did that as a game not so much as direct learning . . . . Around about seven or eight [years old], he said to us, 'I want you to take a round.' . . . and maybe that will be all for a year.

As a logging contractor, he went up the hill and he'd invite us as youngsters . . . to be with him. We need not do anything . . . but I imagine his purpose was for us to watch him do things—how to cut a log so it will fall a certain way. (CHARLIE: 2)

For some people, particularly those who had large families and who did not go to school until the age of nine or ten, the work was more arduous.

. . . Coming from a large family, we all had chores to do as soon as we were able to pick up anything and then there was always a baby. Being the oldest . . . there I was at the age of seven, six . . .

already babysitting . . . . I even helped doing the diapers and feeding the baby . . . . And then we worked out in the garden, we packed wood, we done all these chores. (JOSEPHINE: 2)

Sam, who started at residential school in 1958 at the age of ten, reported that his mother kept him out of school so that he could help with all his little brothers. He was also expected to help with all the household chores including washing clothes and doing dishes. Yet he remembered this time as a time of freedom. Although his memories may be influenced by his early life in contrast to the oppressive system to which he was later subjected, these emotions remain strong in his mind.

For a few, life before school was not all security. Particularly in the 1950s, the influence of alcohol and the coming to parenthood of a generation of people, who through attendance at the residential school had little opportunity to learn parenting skills, created some unhealthy situations for children.

> My mom used to leave us, eh, and this one time she left us with this sitter. At the time, I used to trust everybody and this time she left me with her uncle to babysit us . . . . My mom and dad wanted to go to the dance so they left and this uncle of hers, he . . . sexually abused me. I got to a point where I forgot about it and well I guess I hated the thoughts so much, I just forgot. I remembered after and I didn't know whether I should tell my parents. I was really ashamed. (ALICE: 5)

In what is now understood as the typical reaction of an abused child, this person felt that she must somehow be responsible for the betrayal of trust of the adult in charge. But incidents such as this one were rarely mentioned by the people recalling their lives before school. The emphasis was on a combination of freedom to play and chores to be done.

Grandmothers, as already mentioned, played a major role in educating the children. Traditionally, grandparents were teachers of the community as a whole and the children in particular; to this day, elders are respected as teachers.

> I felt good when I was with my grandmother. I felt like I was with nature and I felt like I was with something that was rightfully mine.
>
> She taught me about nature, about myself, about my Indianness. She taught me all these things and I think that gave me a lot of courage to be where I am today . . . .

The grandmother's teachings were very patient, you know . . . .
I was taught how to make moccasins at an early age of eight and I
knew in later years my first pair of moccasins wasn't the best. But
my grandmother praised me and told me, she says, 'You just
continue . . . . You are going to do better at it each time.' Her
beliefs of teachings was you try to do it on your own, try to think
for yourself. Thinking back now, she was trying to tell me something . . . and I kept on trying . . . because I had so much love for
my grandmother and great-grandmother . . . . I wanted to do more
for them. (MARTHA: 16)

Along with the lessons and encouragement came other attri-
butes of grandmother.

In the winter months, we loved staying with our grandmother
because grandmothers have a habit of collecting a lot of goodies.
I remember my grandmother used to have a box in the corner. We
were not allowed to touch it. We were obedient; we never touched
it because we knew we were going to get it anyway.
    And we were never hungry with my grandmother. If we were
exceptionally good . . . she would reward us with the thing that I
loved—that fruit leather. She used to pick wild raspberries, huckleberries, oh any soft fruits. She'd take it and mash it and, by this
time, she had tin plates, pour it in tin plates and set it out in the
hot sun. It would form a crust on top and then she would flip it
over and it would form a crust on the other side, no sugar added
to it. The inside would form into like a jelly and then she'd put
them away . . . . What she used to do was break a piece off for us
and, boy, we used to just love it. (SOPHIE: 6)

Always there were lessons to be learned. Some came wrapped
in legends, some came as encouragement to attempt a task, and
some as cultural niceties developed through centuries of interaction with other Shuswap people.

My granny was forever, every time she went visiting her relatives
or family, she always came back with bundles of goodies. And
when her friends would come to visit her, she'd give them stuff
. . . . That was one of the traditions that when you went to visit
your friend or your relative, you never left empty-handed. It was
the idea of the nice feeling about giving . . . . The person you give
it to respected you even if she might have loads and loads of dried
saskatoons or huckleberries or whatever, but it was the idea. It

wasn't in big, large packages; it was in just little packages. It was
the idea that you're going with a little gift; you're taking something
from that person . . . . Anyway, that was the type of thing that I
learned when I was young. (SOPHIE: 6)

These traditions were ingrained before the children went to
school and were part of what contributed to the survival of the
Shuswap people despite the onslaught they experienced in a
large part through residential school training. Another, Charlie,
now a teacher, recalls important methodology he learned from
his grandmother.

I had a grandmother who lived with us while our mother and
father were away . . . . She was crippled . . . so she would, from her
bedside, tell us, 'Fill the water three quarters full. Turn the
potatoes now to this level. Make fire.' She provided that knowledge and we just carried out the directions. But, at the same time,
when it was cooked and well done, we'd say, 'Oh, I cooked,' and
that indirect way of learning was good because we were not doing
it as a task, but we were doing it to help grandmother as if we were
in some kind of partnership . . . .

Next week, she would go out. She loved to go out for little walks
and she would say, 'Do you think you can handle cooking up to
the end?' And I'd say, 'Yes, I can.' Oh, if we made the odd mistake,
she'd come and fix it up. It gave us the security to go in there and
do the best possible job we can. Generally, we were 70 to 80%
correct and she would recognize the 80% and not really focus on
the 20% too much. That was her task; the 20% was hers to go in
there and fix it up . . . . My younger brother would at times bake
and his proficiency level was 50%, but he felt good because Grandmother focused on the 50%. She'd say, 'You did good up to this
point. The rest is my job. I'll fix it up.' (3)

The emphasis on children being in a position to observe tasks
which were traditional to their life work was another important
method used by the Shuswap. Young children went along and
played but at the same time began the duty of learning first by
observing and later by doing.

I went everywhere with her [my grandmother]. And so by going
everywhere with her I was learning . . . . I think that was really
where my education started . . . . I picked berries with her. I don't

> remember doing it yet I went with her, but she picked the berries and I goofed around, you know . . . .
>
> I may have watched her more than once do that in the ground cooking, that steam cooking, but I remember that one time that I watched her, I don't even think that I watched 100%. I remember looking for the rocks and her piling up all the things she was going to need, but I think when she was actually cooking the food, I must have been playing somewhere, but I remember eating it. (MARY: 10)

Mary's grandmother died when she was seven and she was subsequently sent to residential school. Clearly, these were the introductory lessons which could have been built upon as the child grew. In an extremely gentle way, the child was made aware of places to pick berries and ways to prepare and cook food. Sophie remembers an incident on a root-digging trip with her grandmother.

> We used to go with her digging roots . . . . She had this mare that had this little colt and she'd take the mare and she'd put all our bedding on the back of the mare and all of her baskets and all our food that we're going to take and maybe camp overnight. So we'd go with her. And ever since that colt was born, we used to handle it. It was so tame; as it grew bigger, we used to grab it. My grandma would be walking along with her cane, leading the horse and we'd be running behind. And we would catch the little colt and we'd hang onto it, all three of us, and the colt was trying to get away. We'd wait until she got quite a ways and one of us would get on and hang on for dear life. That little colt would run to beat heck till soon it would catch up to its mother and she would stop with a jolt and over we'd go. (7)

Both the root digging expedition and the initial steps in riding and training horses were skills which might prove useful in adult life. Neil, in his forties, reminiscing about his life before residential school, recounts that there were always plenty of horses to ride. This point he remembers above all others. Again that which might be expected to be important in adult life was introduced at an early age. For this man, horses have turned out to be his main occupation in life. Horses and horsemanship continue to be valued by and valuable to many Shuswap people today.

Bedtime, always an important time for little children and of seldom discussed cultural significance, was a happy time—a communal time. The hay and mint grass mattress in grandmother's one room cabin has already been described. Linda, in her late thirties, had this to say about bedtime.

> . . . at home we only had two bedrooms. So the boys all slept in one bed and the girls all slept in another bed. And Mum and Dad and whatever the baby was slept in Mum and Dad's room. So we were never, ever separate from one another. We done everything together, slept together, everything . . . (12)

For some, the Catholic religion had already begun to play a major role in their lives. Partly because of the many similarities to traditional Shuswap religion and partly because of effective missionary work on the part of the Oblates, Catholicism had quickly gained a foothold in much of the central region of the province.

> I knew all about the Church . . . . My mum and dad were religious people; they were God-fearing people . . . . Before I went to school, I was already taught there was a God. My mum would point out a lot of things [and say], 'You know, there is definitely a God.' (JOSEPHINE: 2)

Another student, Charlie, recalls:

> The old priest referred to the ground right under us as his text book, as his catechism . . . he would just sit us down, sometimes we'd kneel on the floor or sometimes on his knee. He would say, 'See the water, see the birds, see the sky, see the mountains. View each one because they were made by a greater being than us' . . . . And then he went into hurting and not hurting one another . . . . Of course, these too were taught by our chiefs . . . . One of the stock talks they would give would be to give thanks to the Creator for giving us the water, the trees, all the plants and animals and all the resources of the earth: that they couldn't be made by man, that they had to be made by higher beings than us. (11)

For the young children, these priests seem to have de-emphasized the concepts of guilt, confession and forgiveness, which continue to play prominently in Catholicism. Some informants spoke positively of the formal religion which they experienced before residential school. Most failed to focus on religion and no one spoke negatively of their experience with it before school.

Discipline employed by Shuswap parents and grandparents did prove significant to most of the people with whom I spoke. Generally it included a minimum of physical violence and most frequently was depicted as mild, but fair and effective.

> If you had chores to do . . . you had better get them done. My mum very seldom gave us the strap. We just went back and done them and you just stayed there until you had finished them. (JOSEPHINE: 2)

Even grandparents who were a little frightening did not resort to physical abuse.

> My grandfather used to get mad at my mum and dad all the time, because our parents left us with them so much. They got mad at us too, you know; they got tired of us . . . . I was really afraid of my grandpa then 'cause he used to holler lots . . . . No, they never spanked any of us. My grandma was really nice though. (ALICE: 11)

Anne, raised by her grandmother, recalled that on only one occasion had her grandmother punished her severely. She had gone to the washroom without her grandmother's permission during a community dance and was fascinated by an older girl putting on lipstick, " . . . when all of a sudden, 'Whack! Whack!' and there was my grandmother just tugging me out the door" (5).

After destroying a number of plants in a greenhouse, Mary reported that when her mother demanded a reason from her, she responded that she had done it because she wanted to. Because she was honest, she " . . . never got a lickin' or anything. I didn't do it because I hated him or hated her or anything. I [just] wanted to" (5). In another incident, Mary describes what may be seen as the adult consequences of her behaviour.

> Another time the same guy, he was teasing me and I was across the heater and there was a poker there for the heater. He was teasing me and I was mad . . . . I said, 'I'll hit you with this.' I took the poker and he said, 'Go ahead. Go ahead.' And I did. I went like this [gesturing]. 'Boink.' He didn't think I would and I did. He looks at my mum and my mum never said anything. Finally, he said, 'Aren't you going to do something about it?' My mum said,

'What can I do? She told you she was going to hit you; you said to go ahead.' (5)

Interesting to note is that the person engaged in the altercation with the child was non-Native. Clearly, he did not understand that children in Shuswap culture were viewed as young adults in many ways, and that under these circumstances, he had made an error in judgement.

These stories highlight the important memories of home life before school for people who were all destined for the Kamloops Indian Residential School. Some of the carefree nature of life before the residential school may be attributed to the fact that, without exception, the children were no more than ten years of age and therefore had limited responsibility. However, the tenor of a life closely connected with the natural world, the importance of the grandmother's presence and teachings which in many cases continued to influence the children into adulthood, and the assumption that children are full-fledged contributing members of the household stand out as extremely important in the lives of these Shuswap children.

Of particular significance is the resultant clash of these cultural notions with the systematized, European-influenced life at the residential school. The rigid time schedules, the dearth of family contact even amongst siblings, and the constant supervision and direction accompanied by severe punishments for deviation were aspects of a way of life foreign to Shuswap children.

THE TRANSITION

Into the idyllic summer life of camping and berry and root gathering came the school truck. Out stepped a huge European man in black clothing with a list in his hand. The separation began.

> The school truck used to come with a little fence around the back, you know. Used to come, I think for Chase, it was August 30th or was it the 31st? Anyway, they had me ready. My mum brought me and everybody grouped around the truck. And I think it was Anthony Liah would have a list of names and you went on up these little stairs as your name was called. (MARY: 1)

Most people now refer to this truck as the cattle truck, but at

that time it was called the school truck. For many children, it
was their initial introduction to a way of life in which their family
identity was obscured, their language became useless and even
despised, and their personal identification was a number written in purple ink on their wrists and on the small cupboard in
which their few belongings were stored. Not all stops were as
orderly as the one described above. For some students, the
resistance to a new culture began with that initial contact. Linda
described these horrific scenes:

> I can remember Dad left really early that morning 'cause he never,
> ever wanted to see us go off to school. And when he left that
> morning at five, I tried sneaking out with him. He was really
> crying, my dad was. And he told me, 'No, you stay. You got to go
> to school.' And I just [said], 'No, I want to stay with you. I want to
> stay with you.' And I was crying just as hard as he was. Finally, I
> just wrapped my arms and legs right around him and every time
> he went to take a step, he had to pack me with him 'cause I was
> hanging on to him so hard. He walked back in the house and
> pulled me off of him and sat me on the couch and he finally yelled
> at me, 'You sit right there and don't you move until them people
> come.' But he was crying. He walked out and he got on his horse
> and went and left. That was really hard to take, you know . . . .
>
> When that truck did come, boy, I tell you. We had a back door
> and a front door and we beelined it. I didn't know exactly where
> they were going, but when everybody started running, I started to
> run too and realized that the truck was there. And they literally
> chased us down . . . .
>
> And the kids that are on the truck, they're all bawling because
> they're seeing us, you know, screaming and yelling . . . . Of course,
> they're all crying because we're crying and Mum's crying and I can
> remember [saying], 'What'd I ever do to you? Why are you mad at
> me? Why are you sending me away?' . . . . She was really heartbro-
> ken. (21)

The confusion and distress on the part of both parents and
children were clear. The painful process of cultural invasion,
the first step of which involved removing the children from the
influence of their parents, had begun.

Although the 'cattle truck' was the most frequently
remembered travelling conveyance, some children came to

school using other means. Cecilia, who attended in 1907, recalled:

> When our people bring us back to school, they go on the wagon a few days ahead. And they camp close to the river, on this side of the bridge. Lots of 'em do that. They got no car, just go on a wagon or a buggy. Take lots of lunch. When it's time to go back to school, they bring you to the school, the Indian school. (5)

Certainly, this trip to school provided a temporary stay to the impending attack on the child's way of life by the agents of the government and church. Sophie remembered going to school by car.

> . . . out of the blue there comes this car, drove up to my mother and father's place. And my mother was dressing up my sister and I . . . and my mother told us that we were going to be riding in that car . . . and that we were going to go to school. We didn't know what a school was. I thought maybe we'd go there and come right back. And that was the most terrifying part of my whole life. It seemed like that car chugged along forever . . . . It took us seemed like a whole day and it seemed like we were gone to the other end of the world and we'd never find our way home. (8)

Sophie's story of fear is made more poignant when one knows that, following an incident much discussed in hushed tones by the adults of the community, she had been warned to run if she ever saw a white man. Suddenly she found herself in a car with a strange European person going she knew not where. The incident, she heard years later, had involved the rape of a young Native woman by three European men. The woman's baby, which had been strapped to her back, had been smothered during the encounter.

For other children, the day for going to school was a time of pleased anticipation. New clothes brought great excitement to Alice's introduction to school in the 1950s.

> What used to happen is our parents used to buy new clothes and then we were sent to school . . . . I think we went over on the bus and I was kind of looking forward to this 'cause we're going on this trip with our brand new clothes. My sisters never even told me what it was like there . . . they never talked about the school. And I wondered what it was going to be like. It was almost like a

celebration coming up . . . . That was the greatest thing to have new clothes. (1)

Frequently the children who went to school willingly were older—nine or ten years and they usually had some understanding that although their parents would miss them dreadfully, learning to read and write was of prime importance.

> My mum explained to me, when we discussed it . . . she said, 'I'm sending you to learn to read and write and to learn your catechism, to learn about God' . . . . So I knew why I was coming to school.
>
> My cousin Eliza was appointed to bring me . . . . I was apprehensive. I was wondering how it was going to be. I knew I was leaving my mum . . . but we had discussed it so many times before and it was happening, you know, it was real. But I guess with Eliza, on the bus, she just had such a hard time to keep from crying. (MARY: 2)

Two points of significance arise in this story. The first is the fact that the child's mother had never attended residential or any school and Eliza had. Because she understood what lay ahead for the child, Eliza felt some trepidation. The mother, on the other hand, recognized that some good could come of learning to read and write, which she saw as the goals of the school. Secondly, the children whose parents explained the purpose of the school to them felt more comfortable with their journey to school. In traditional education, these complex explanations were unnecessary because education was part of the natural flow of life. With the cultural onslaught of the residential school, parents were required to make a major adjustment to their way of dealing with their children in order to smooth the transition into a foreign culture. Only for some was this need recognized.

With arrival at the school, the cultural attacks began in earnest. Some of the clashes were deliberate, a part of the Oblates' plan and the government's mandate to 'civilize and Christianize' the Native people. Others, which may have been well intentioned, demonstrated the lack of cultural awareness and sensitivity of the people in charge of the children. More than any other time at the school, the memories of the first day live vividly in the minds of every person interviewed.

> Coming to this huge, huge building, it staggered us. With eight of

us in a home and sometimes ten, we lived in a one room house
. . . . It seemed, as we came into the building, we were just swal-
lowed up by some strange being. Everything was strange, even the
running water was strange. The bathroom was strange. The echo
of the hallway was a noise I hadn't heard before and the banging
of doors from far away was strange. We came into a totally strange
world. (CHARLIE: 1)

Sophie, another student, remembered this scene:

All of a sudden, here we come in front of this building. And after
being told to be afraid of white people, you can imagine the feeling
we had. We were herded into the front and down the hall where
the dining room is. We were all standing there: my sister and I
hanging on to each other. We were already so scared and we were
lonely for the protection of our parents. We didn't know what we
were going to be getting into. [We wondered], 'Why did my
mother and father send us away?'

And then, all of a sudden, we seen somebody coming down the
hallway all in black and just this white face and that's when I started
just shaking and we all started crying and backing up . . . . We were
doing that of sheer fright. This sister is coming towards us and
what has been going in her mind is, 'Here's these little wild
animals.' You know when you go to touch a little wild animal, it
cringes and we say right away, 'Oh, it's a wild animal. We've got
to tame it.' I could just imagine what was going on in her mind,
'These little wild Indians: I've got to tame them.' . . . . And here
me, I'm saying, 'I'm so scared. What is she going to do to me?'
And after hearing about them killing our own people, 'Are they
here to butcher us or what are they going to do to us?' (8)

The school personnel's perception of Indian children as wild
and animal-like is supported by comments made by the Oblates
regarding their efforts to instill European values into the minds
of the Native people. The first close up view of the nuns brought
fear to many children.

I just couldn't get over these nuns wearing long black . . . . I was
kind of scared of them; they looked so white. They had this little
part of their face showing, everything else was covered . . . their
long beads rattled. When they walked, their little heels clicked on
the cement floor. Wherever they went, you could hear them
walking because they had that heel and the little jangle. (ALICE: 8)

Strange sights and strange sounds filled the children's first days of school.

Although many children came to the school in tears, the more defiant ones were dragged kicking and screaming from the truck.

> . . . the first day I went to that school, they had to literally carry me off the truck and that nun, I have her outfit in shambles. I was calling her a witch and just kicking and screaming at her. I mean I wasn't the only one; there was a lot of other kids that were doing that and finally the head nun . . . she had the strap and she went, 'Whack! Whack!' on the table . . . . 'Okay, you kids,' she said, 'That's enough out of you or you're going to get this.' (LINDA: 12)

For children who had rarely experienced physical punishment, the threat of the strap must have seemed especially fearsome.

Once in the school, students were often subjected to head checks for lice before the mandatory haircuts.

> We had to get in this line and we had to get our heads checked for lice . . . . Some of the kids had to get their heads cleaned. And soon as they finished checking our heads, they cut our hair. They cut our hair in front like bangs above the eyebrows, side to side on your face here by the temples . . . and just right at the top part of your ear, it was cut straight around and on the back where your neck is, it was cut so straight that the back parts here were shaved . . . . I think we practically all looked the same 'cause we all had the same haircut, the same coloured clothes and all had the same everything. (ALICE: 1)

Along with the initial shock and fear of leaving their parents and entering into a strange world, the hair cut added salt to their wounds. Traditionally, the styling of females' long hair had played a role in important events, including puberty rites. Cutting hair short had been used as punishment for adult women for offenses such as adultery. Although the hair cutting may not have had overt cultural significance for those who attended the school in later years, many parents maintained the tradition of leaving girls' hair uncut. The other concern expressed by the informant dealt with a feeling of loss of personal identity at a very sensitive time as children realized that they now 'all looked the same.'

For those with family members and friends already attending

the school, one would expect that their support might ease the transition from home into school. As has already been mentioned, frequently siblings and friends did not discuss their school experiences at home. Presumably the pain of school was a topic to be avoided during time away. Built into the rigid structure of the school were segregations which severely limited access to other family members. Whether this was done intentionally, as a means of continuing the assault on the strong family ties which might permit the maintenance of cultural traits, or whether it was merely a matter of convenience for the staff, remains unclear.

The children were divided into three age groups: juniors for grades one to three, intermediates for grades four to six, and seniors for grades seven and eight. There was little social interaction permitted amongst the groups. Nancy recalled her sister's first day at the school.

> ... I remember her really, really getting scared. You know, she was excited at the beginning, at home, feeling safe, having safe surroundings and then from there she was taken with us on the bus all the way down here .... Her and I had to go in separate parts of the building so I remember her clinging onto my arms when we were going up the stairs ... and she kept telling me in Chilcotin she didn't want to go .... She didn't know English very much and the sisters yanked her away because I had to go to my room ....
>
> I remember feeling very sorry for her and feeling like I couldn't help her very much, feeling helpless. I felt like I was put in a position to look out for her, but that didn't take form because she couldn't spend a week with me to adjust to the whole thing—me telling her exactly what the routine was. But they didn't think of that; they didn't think of Indian kids' interests I don't think. (11)

Other people recollected knowing that their sisters were in a room beside them but that they could not visit one another. This separation of family members sometimes resulted in a feeling of powerlessness as expressed by the older sister above. For the Oblates' purposes and in the light of traditional European schooling this sense of powerlessness was appropriate to children who were seen as mere objects to be subjected to the treatment deemed fitting for them by their elders and betters. Of course, this approach is in direct contrast to the traditional

Shuswap view that children were in many senses fully participating members of a household. The process which created this feeling of impotence is reiterated in the following:

> Before I left [home], I was full of confidence: I could do everything that was needed to be done at home . . . . But when I arrived here all that left me. I felt so helpless. The Shuswap language was no use to me . . . the supervisors couldn't understand. (CHARLIE: 1)

For Mary, as an older child coming to school, this sense of helplessness was triggered by her first cultural clash. Her initial hours at the school had been relatively comfortable: "I have no emotions yet and, you know, it's all new and I have to keep my eyes open and learn." This healthy interest came to a rude end after the first supper.

> After supper, everybody had jobs . . . . And I'm standing there, you know, [thinking], 'Where's everybody going? What's happening?' And this sister called me and said, 'You're new; you go to the recreation room.' And I have no idea what the recreation room is and I'm standing there . . . . Now there is the first emotion I had. 'What is she saying?' And she calls, 'Clara, come here.' So I looked back and here this little girl comes bouncing towards sister. 'Clara, you take Mary down to the recreation room and then you come back and do your work.' And this little girl takes my hand, smaller than me, she's so bouncy and happy looking, she takes me and I'm dying of shame that this little girl knows what this big word is and she knows where she is going to. Holy man, I mean what's the matter with me? Oh, I'm so ashamed. She takes me to the recreation room and says, 'This is the recreation room,' and she smiles at me and she leaves. And I go in there. I guess there are some more of us big dummies . . . . (3)

Although intended to be helpful, the sister's action violated a social rule. To be helped by someone obviously smaller and younger in front of other people was public humiliation. To this day, losing face publicly is seen by many Shuswap people as a terrible insult; to that child on that day so long ago, the action was devastating.

Not only were older and younger siblings separated, but in the spirit of old Catholicism, males and females were isolated from one another. Sexuality has often been viewed by conservative factions within the Catholic Church as an area which may lead to sin. Initially, it resulted in the separation of brothers and sisters. More than one student reported seeing her brother once or not at all during years of attendance at the school.

The introduction to life on the boys' side was seen by most study participants as very rough.

> The first night I had three scraps on account of my brothers. You always got tested out. I showed them . . . . I was more out-going, ready for anything on account of my [public] schooling over there. (SAM: 8)

The boys' resistance to the system being imposed upon them took a different form from the girls', which tended to be more subtle but just as effective. In the action of fighting the rules and regulations of the school, they also developed a counter-culture of clique-like groupings sometimes based loosely on reservation origins. Some boys who arrived later in September than the others ("I suppose they looked at their list, saw there was still room at the school, and they went back and got us"), found their introduction very trying.

> Do you know when we see pictures of musk ox in a circle being attacked by wolves . . . it seemed we were that . . . we were in the center—four of us. Youngsters of all ages touching us and watching our reactions as we tried to grab or scratch or hit. As our backs were turned, somebody would grab us from the back. And we just wished we could return home to a more safe and secure place. (CHARLIE: 1)

Examination of the groupings which developed amongst the boys in their daily life at the school suggests that this initiation was part of the process of screening newcomers to determine their toughness. According to several informants, this type of behaviour was not typical of children's interactions at home, but was produced by the oppressive atmosphere of the school. One girl's brother had been to the school before her and he apparently tried to prepare his siblings for the treatment which they could be subjected to on arrival at school.

> My oldest brother, he wanted to prepare us for our life. Like he was teaching us how to fight and he taught us that we shouldn't cry if something happened to us . . . . He wanted us to be tough. (ALICE: 15)

This type of behaviour at home was described only by Alice; no other informants reported such cases.

Language, that aspect of culture so central to its expression and transmission, was a major issue within the school. With obvious understanding of the importance of eliminating this tool of culture, the Oblates began their attack on the Native languages during the children's first days at school and continued to escalate the conflict with those who did not co-operate in abandoning their language. For the children who spoke only Shuswap on their arrival at school, their first days were ones of gibberish because older children were not permitted to speak the language and few supervisors ever spoke Shuswap. No transition time in which they might reach some understanding of the system before being asked to learn a new language was alotted. One nine year old remembered:

> And knowing very little English, I had some difficulty with that. I got into trouble because of not knowing English and not speaking out or saying the wrong word, even being confused about yes and no . . . . One of the supervisors wrote our names and our numbers: we each had a school number on our wrist. So rather than answering in English, 'What is your number? What is your name?' . . . we would just show our wrist . . . . That was our identification; they wrote it in that purple pencil. (CHARLIE: 34)

For some, the first day of school was too full of new experiences for language to have been a major focus: one person who did speak English reported, "I don't think I did very much talking the first few days 'cause, you know, you had to get used to everything around here."

The final shock of the first day came at bedtime. Instead of the communal beds of home, the children were directed to dormitories containing rows and rows of individual beds with white sheets and a single blanket. For a few, this time meant happiness: "What I remember the most was getting into a bed of my own and it had clean sheets. The place smelled great" *(Sophie: 1)*. Sam described his first night very differently: he recalls standing at the window holding his two brothers' hands as they cried and gazed longingly toward their nearby home on the Kamloops Reserve. "I kept looking over there—freedom, what I used to do" *(Sam: 2)*. For another person, the sheets and pillow offered little solace.

When they tried to put me to bed without my sister, in this one bed with my own pillow, my own sheet, I didn't even think that was very nice. I couldn't believe that I didn't have nobody to sleep with. That I was going to have a bed all to myself sort of scared me and I howled all night. (LINDA: 12)

Again no recognition was given to the Shuswap ways and no allowance for gradual introduction of European conventions was permitted. In a systematic and rigid fashion, the Oblates demonstrated that the Shuswap cultural patterns were not acceptable in the school. In all aspects of life, from language to sleeping habits, European behaviours were to supplant those which had been followed by generations of Shuswap people. From these first days, no concessions were made: family ties were broken, language use was forbidden, and life experiences discounted.

As this oppressive system began to operate, glimmerings of a developing counter-culture were also in evidence. In subtle and not so subtle ways, the children began the delicate balancing act of adaptation to a new order while retaining the indelible aspects of their original culture. This resistance to the system which resulted in the production of sub-cultures within the school began on the first days. The following example typifies the underground culture in operation.

I had to sneak to my sister's bed. She was in the same dorm as I was. I don't know who the girls were who were sleeping beside us but they were going to squeal on us and she up and told them she'd beat the living shit right out of them if they so much as said a word. She was classified as one of the tough girls so they listened to her. (LINDA: 12-13)

While cultural invasion had begun in earnest, the forces of opposition were also forming ranks. It is this strength of resistance which has ensured the survival of the Shuswap people as a nation today despite the efforts of both governments and missionaries to undermine their cultural roots and have them become an indistinguishable part of the dominant society. Although its effects have been devastating for individuals, the Kamloops Indian Residential School was not successful in its attempts to assimilate the Native people of the Central Interior of the province.

CHAPTER 3
SCHOOL LIFE

"Thus, at the inception of the Indian School question, we find two main characteristics which have ever since continued, i.e. the principal of the per capita grant and the denominational interest."
Unsigned letter, 1908 (B.C. Archives)

In recalling their time at the Kamloops Indian Residential School, people shared memories which could be categorized in three ways: general details of their daily lives, specific sensational incidents, and their current impressions of what happened there based on the two former types of memories and their subsequent life experience. The three intertwine with one another and in so doing provide fascinating insights into the effects which the school had. Leo reported thus:

> To me, the Indian school generally speaking was sort of like you were taken over by a superior force, by the government and [they] try to mold you into something else and they were very strict about it . . . . (12)

Martha had similar recollections:

> At the Indian residential school, we were not allowed to speak our language; we weren't allowed to dance, sing because they told us it was evil. It was evil for us to practice any of our cultural ways . . . .
>
> Some of the girls would get some Indian food . . . . They'd take it away from us and just to be mean they'd destroy it right in front of us. You know, that's how bad it was. (9)

Although there was some change over time, Indian culture was never accepted by the school as a real, living culture. Rather it was seen as something archaic and undesirable, something to be annihilated. As the dominant culture gathered strength and it perceived that Indian culture was indeed dying, there was noticeable relaxation in what was allowed in the school. An examination of daily life accents these claims and demonstrates

58

clearly the systematic destruction of culture which was attempted.

THE SCHOOL DAY

Morning came early for the students attending the Kamloops Indian Residential School in the 1930s.

> In the morning, we had to get up at six o'clock, perfect silence. We all took turns going into the bathroom: we'd fill our basin full of water and we'd take it to our bedside. We'd wash, take that basin, empty it, clean it out, put it back, fix our bed, get dressed and as soon as you're finished—you only had half an hour to do all this—brush your teeth, get in a line and stand in line in perfect silence. If you're caught ever speaking one word, boy, you got cuffed around.
>
> And then we marched from there down to the chapel and we spent over an hour in the chapel every morning, every blessed morning. And there they interrogated us on what it was all about being an Indian . . . . He would just get so carried away; he was punching away at that old altar rail . . . to hammer it into our heads that we were not to think or act or speak like an Indian. And that we would go to hell and burn for eternity if we did not listen to their way of teaching. (SOPHIE: 9)

What better way to work at indoctrination than to take hungry children early in the morning and to subject them to a harangue on the evils of their family's way of life. It certainly appears to be an impelling way to create change. No attempt was made at dialogue or reaching common understanding. Complete silence of the 'objects' being addressed ensured little opportunity for the children to put the attack into a context which might enable them to understand more fully the words directed at them. They had no opportunity to question the priest and no opportunity to speak to one another about what they had heard. Those who were caught speaking to one another were quickly punished.

> Oh, in church when the girls were laughing . . . somebody must be watching. Just grab them by the neck, make them lay down on the floor till after church. (CECILIA: 2)

Of course, the Mass at this time was given in Latin. Not only were the children expected to learn English, they were also exposed to a third language in church.

In later years, daily attendance at Mass was no longer mandatory. One of the benefits for those who were involved in sports or dancing was that they were excused from the daily chapel service on occasion. However, those who chose not to attend the voluntary services often found themselves assigned extra cleaning duties during the Mass time. Following chapel, the children again moved in ranks to the dining room. Staff ate in a separate nearby room. Eventually, a partition was constructed down the centre of the dining room so that the sexes could not view one another during meals.

Almost everyone interviewed mentioned the infamous porridge served every morning at the Kamloops Indian Residential School. Prepared by students, with only minimal supervision by the nuns or older students, it was described most often as lumpy and burnt. Josephine, who had been involved in preparing the porridge, described it this way:

> We had some pretty good cooks there and some pretty bad cooks . . . . When you make porridge in those great big pots . . . you learned that porridge is to be cooked in boiling water and a bit of salt and that you stir it so that it doesn't burn on the bottom . . . . Well, if they cook it in just warm water and not boiling water, you can be sure it's going to be sticky because that porridge sits there all night . . . . If you have to, then you add a little more hot water in the morning. You know, that's one thing that sticks in my mind is this sticky porridge. (5)

The porridge even became the focus of small gestures of resistance. Unfortunately, those who refused to eat it found it waiting for them at the next meal as was the case with all rejected food. Others found the porridge a source of entertainment in an otherwise mundane morning meal.

> I used to get a kick out of that when I think back. We used to have this habit [to see] who could stretch the porridge the longest. We'd take our spoon and we'd start tapping the porridge up and down. Finally we'd get it going like a long string of gum and we'd see who could get it the longest. And we'd get caught and, boy, did we ever get a licking. (SOPHIE: 10)

She went on to point out that the children usually ate it.

> You know, when you're hungry, you'll eat anything. They put a

blob of that [mush] in our plate, a piece of bread, a little bit of butter and a glass of blue milk. (SOPHIE: 10)

Meals were served by the children themselves and at least one person felt there was some justification for the unappetizing food.

I forget how many kids there was when I was going there. Imagine trying to cook for them. You couldn't put [the food] into individual platters and make it look appetizing. You know, there had to be a big pot at the end of that table . . . [with] those eight children—eight on each side of the table and one serves. (JOSEPHINE: 5)

The dominant impression of mealtime is a sense of regimentation. Individuality here and at other times was not a concern. The numbers of children who had to be fed were seen as objects to be processed as cheaply and efficiently as possible, then passed along to the next station.

Another source of concern to those interviewed was the inequity between the staff's food and the children's. Those who worked in the kitchen were most aware of the differences. One person suggested that the method of preparation provided the greatest disparity. Rather than being cooked ahead of time in huge vats, the staff's meals were prepared just before serving. Others described in detail the tasty and nutritious food which they saw being delivered to the staff dining room. Nancy, who attended in the sixties, commented on the double standard she felt was expressed in the inequity.

For them it was different . . . . They didn't eat the same food we ate; they ate much better food. We had mush and they had bacon and eggs. They were separate from everybody else in one room where the whole staff ate. (5)

This discrimination was mentioned by several people. The sense of injustice caused by the varying quality of the food was intensified when students watched the meals being taken into the staff room as they were going into their less satisfying meal.

Many people remember hunger. George Manuel, in his book *The Fourth World*, names hunger as the first of three things which stand out in his mind about school. One of the participants in this study, Leo, reported:

Something I remember was that I was always hungry. I lost weight

there. I gained ten to twelve pounds in two months at home. I go
down there and I lose two or three in ten months. (11)

This child was, of course, growing. That some of his weight
increase in summer was growth-related makes even more significant the subsequent loss during the time at school. During the
ten months, he would have been growing while actually losing
weight.

Following a less than satisfactory breakfast and the morning
cleaning duties, the children moved to the classroom block. For
the newcomers, more adjustments were necessary on their
introduction to another unknown.

> Our first day we went to the classroom. They had all these little
> desks lined up; I think there were about thirty or thirty-five seats
> in this little room, maybe more . . . . So this nun was there; she was
> our teacher. I still wasn't used to looking at these people . . . . We
> were going into this classroom two by two and they just told us to
> sit down so we got to pick any place. And some kids were coming
> in that day [who] were really scared. The little girls were so scared
> they were crying really loud . . . . The girls were kicking and
> screaming and two older students were holding them by the arms,
> trying to bring them in . . . . And that scared the rest of us, 'cause
> we were so small sitting there wondering, 'What's going on? Why
> are we here?' And day after day, we went back there and it took
> us a long time to get to know each other. (ALICE: 3)

A child who started school at nine years of age remembered her
awkwardness on that first day:

> You know when you first enter the room, you'd never seen desks
> before . . . . You were just like cattle. And these kids that were
> there . . . were laughing at us, you know . . . . We were the same
> age, but they'd been in school before . . . . And they were our own
> people saying these things. (MARY: 4)

The first hour of classroom time was devoted to religious
training. Although assimilation was the government's prime
objective for the Indian people, the Oblates had as their goal,
"the development of a child's character in accordance with the
true concept of Christian education" *(Cronin: 223)*. For some
of the students, in retrospect, this concept as interpreted by
their teachers was of questionable worth.

I remember when we were in the school there that all other churches were wrong. If you believed or read any of the other books, you were going to hell. That was pushed into our brain day after day after day at school. Didn't matter what church, what religion . . . the Catholic was the only church. There was no other church, absolutely. (LEO: 12)

For others, religion became like any other class.

It just started to be like arithmetic, like reading, being taught catechism while sitting in a row . . . . To me anyways . . . it didn't quite tie in because it went by the bell. It went by strict routine. I guess I missed the personal contact that we started with at home with Granny and with the priest . . . . And so it became like the main text book was the catechism book, always memorizing . . . the Baltimore Catechism. (CHARLIE: 12)

Others recall the sense of guilt which they were expected to develop as a part of their training.

When you're raised a Catholic, everything is wrong that you're doing. At least that was my opinion. If you went to the washroom, that was wrong. If you wiped your ass, that was wrong. If you looked at your private parts, that was wrong . . . . If you talked to this person, it was wrong or if you looked at that person, it was wrong. The whole attitude of the religious upbringing really squashed you. You weren't able to express your true self. Everything was controlled. (ANNE: 12)

Some found that their developing religious sense shattered their image of self and family.

. . . they started talking to us about sin, about what sin was . . . . I felt really dirty 'cause this [sexual abuse] happened to me . . . . They started teaching me their religion . . . telling me who God was, what Hell was and what angels were . . . . They said, ' . . . anybody that doesn't go to church is a pagan.' I started thinking, 'Hey, my parents don't go to church all the time. They must be pagans . . . . ' People that got drunk, they would really put them down. I thought, 'Gee, our family is really the pits.' And I'd go home and I'd be really ashamed of my parents. (ALICE: 10)

Although major celebrations such as First Communion and Confirmation were happy times,

> Those were nice days because we got dressed up so nice, pretty
> dresses. Even the boys got special little clothes, too, (ALICE: 10)

the Sacrament of Penance which preceded Holy Communion
was another matter.

> . . . they wanted us to go to Confession and tell our sins. Well gee,
> I didn't know what kind of sin I was to tell. It was funny standing
> there in line on Saturday; we'd all be in the hall ready to go to
> Confession. So we'd go into these little boxes, eh, and the priest
> would be in there and one girl on the other side and one on this
> side and it was dark . . . . The priest would say, 'Okay, what did you
> do?' or whatever . . . . I used to make up lies and I'd say, 'Oh, I told
> seventeen lies . . . . ' I just made up these things and the priest
> would say, 'Okay, I want you to go and say ten Hail Mary's, five
> Glory Be's and one Our Father.' . . . and we'd go do that . . . .
> (ALICE: 10)

For another student, confession became a time of great tension
when the priest consistently asked her if she had had sexual
relations with anyone. His unseemly interest in the subject
combined with his displays of affection for her which involved
touching her in public led the student to believe that the priest
was making overtures to her. In her family, displays of affection
were minimal. Assuming the priest's intentions were harmless,
his insensitivity to her discomfort was not.

The organized Catholic religion, a renowned force in early
settlement in North America, had a profound effect on every
student who attended the residential school in Kamloops. For
those who had experienced an introduction to Catholicism before leaving home and whose parents had adopted and adapted
the religion as a part of their way of life, the cultural shock of its
teachings had less impact. For others, the values enforced by the
teachings of the religion, particularly the notions of evil, sin,
guilt, and hell fire were foreign and fearsome. The long term
effects of these teachings were many; in some cases they are still
being felt. The use of religion as a weapon in the attack on
traditional Native spirituality and other cultural aspects was
particularly devastating to those individuals whose families were
already struggling with the changes expected of them.

Following the hour of religion each morning, a mere two
hours were dedicated to the academic subjects: basic reading,
arithmetic, and writing, combined with a few other subject areas

such as art and social studies. Although some students felt comfortable with the expectations of them in the classroom, many others found the time threatening and unpleasant.

> We were graded very much as we do today .... There were a lot of slow learners and then the ones that were a little better and then the ones that advanced quite fast and understand better than the others. I think I was about in the middle ....
>
> For no reason, I think, they said, 'You have the brains; you're just lazy. We know you can do it.' And I know I can do it, but oftentimes I got behind and then I stayed behind. (JOSEPHINE: 4)

For this student, school time was full of pressure. She worked hard but when she could not meet expectations, she felt inadequate. The teacher's comments were very different from her mother's directions to go and finish what was left undone. Because the student had always found this punishment enough, the extra severity of the teacher's verbal harangue was damaging to her self-image. On the other hand, many people interviewed found time spent on the academic subjects was quite positive. Specific memories are notable in that they are harder to recall. When probed, the students had comments like this:

> I don't know what we learned. I remember we started learning, I think Joe and Ruth books. We had readers .... I really can't even tell you what we learned. I remember this big book they used to have hanging on the front. It was something about Rover and Bob and those were the words that we learned. And if we were really good with our work ... the teacher would go to the next pages of this great big book with big letters. I liked that .... (MARY: 5)

These students found the academic work challenging and the teachers fair. Regarding her teacher, Mary said:

> I thought she was quite fair. She had worked hard and she was a real teacher you know. She really taught us ....
>
> Oh, I know one of the first things we did .... She gave us papers and pencils and we had to write our name .... I was taught by someone to print my name with capital letters and I could remember working on that. Oh, I was so proud that I could write my name. (6)

Students' general comments about school are best summarized in the initial sentence of the following quotation. Leo is the only one who mentioned work other than reading and arithmetic when discussing the elementary grades.

> You learnt the three R's there, you know, the basics. You learned a little bit about history . . . but there was no history about B.C. . . . . They never taught us why Vancouver was called Vancouver or anything like that. They taught us all about Quebec and French and all the explorers. We learned a bit about South America . . . . We learned about King Henry the Eighth and Fifth and all those guys. (11-12)

Needless to say, no Shuswap history was taught. With the ethnocentric bias of the times, only European-based history was deemed important enough to be taught in schools. Additionally, when a culture is being attacked in an effort to dominate it or to replace it with an alternative way of life, an effective tactic includes lack of acknowledgement of that culture's history.

The most significant aspect of the schooling at the residential school is that, until the late 1940s, no child attended school for longer than two hours a day. The discrepancy between the hours of schooling in residential school and the five hours spent by students in the public school resulted in the inability of most students to transfer into the public school if they had chosen to continue their education after grade eight. In most cases, continuation was not encouraged and was considered inappropriate and unnecessary for Native people. The governments and the missionaries had decided that Native people should be farmers or farmers' wives, not scholars. A person who left school in the 1940s recalled:

> I think once you left there, you're sixteen or seventeen, most of us. When I found out there was going to be no high school . . . we didn't care about education any more. We just wanted to work for a living . . . .
> [The priests] never talked to me at all. Never said, 'How would you like to come back?' or 'We'll make arrangements.' . . . not like nowadays [when they] try to put you ahead . . . . You didn't have any counsellors and the old folks didn't care one way or another. (LEO: 17-18)

Any person who did decide to attempt high school or further education would have been breaking new ground with little support either from people at the residential school or at home.

Not until 1946 was the high school program instituted at the residential school. At that time one student in Kamloops began high school. The following year, five others, carefully selected, joined him. For the first time in their lives, they were expected to attend school from nine to three.

> Then came grade nine. We started high school and we had to go a full day . . . and those teachers had to try and teach us to graduate in four years. We had to write provincial exams. (MARY: 13)

In writing these provincial examinations, students were judged along with those who had been in the public school system for twelve years. The Native students had experienced approximately five public school years during their initial eight years at the residence. The fact that the six original graduates had passed their exams with only the equivalent of nine years of public schooling demonstrated their strong academic ability. This comparison is not emphasized in existing accounts of the early graduates of Kamloops Indian Residential School. To do so would have drawn attention to the inequities of the education system for the Native students.

For students such as these, the time for academic studies was the high point of their day. They tended to be the ones whose parents had explained to them that the purpose for going to school was to learn to read and write. The able students frequently completed the three grade one levels—1c, 1b, and 1a—all in their first year at school.

> I did do all grade 1c, grade 1b and grade 1a [which was] surprising [because] it took me so long to get started. I used to be so nervous about doing my work and wanting to do it so well. I actually punctured my book . . . . I put my pencil right through it—all that muscle tension—trying to get an A or B . . . .
>
> [A] little past mid-year, I began to look at things, 'I know this experience,' . . . and I got interested in matching it with a word that the teacher would have. And having this discovery, 'Carrying water, I've done that.' That's a simple experience that matched what I was doing. Making fire, that's a simple experience, that matched with making fire in words. That drew me: this is exciting; this is fascinating . . . just the mere fascination of matching a previous experience with the actual words. I would think of that after school and looking at a tree, 'I must learn the word for tree.

> I must learn the word for mountain; I must learn the word for
> ground . . . .' (CHARLIE: 8)

Such tremendous self motivation could lead only to success as
a student. Indeed, this person was the first high school graduate
of the Kamloops Indian Residential School.

For other students, general insensitivity to their concerns and
those of their classmates made school time more tumultuous
than it needed to be. One student who transferred to K.I.R.S.
from another residential school was upset by an unexplained
decision that she repeat a year.

> I don't remember how they decided that I was to go back one more
> grade. I was grade two and they put me back in grade one I
> remember thinking that it was negative like maybe I was dumb or
> something like that. I don't remember being told why. They
> immediately put me back in grade one. (NANCY: 10)

The want of an explanation exemplifies the lack of understanding of childhood concerns on the part of the adults in charge.
Another informant reported suffering to this day because of
action taken with a close friend from her reserve.

> The first few days of school what I remember was Betty from our
> reserve was also a newcomer and about four days after we came
> . . . all of a sudden, they packed her up and they sent her home.
> Why, I don't know, you know. And I think, 'She's the same age as
> me. We come from the same place. What's different? . . . . I do not
> understand and I have feelings that somebody should explain it to
> me . . . . Why, who and what made that decision? . . . . I don't know
> why . . . but it hurts me today yet. (MARY: 3)

Again a simple explanation might have sufficed to calm the
child then and through the years. Because she wanted to be at
school, she worried that the same thing might happen to her.
She also worried for her friend and her feelings about having
to leave school. Although this treatment is characteristic of the
treatment of children particularly before the 1960s and even to
the present day, the fact that the school personnel were serving
both as teachers and as surrogate families to children from
another culture might have implied the need for special awareness of potentially upsetting situations. The resultant action
could have allayed the fears of the children involved. A shortage
of staff may have contributed to the inability of those involved

to deal with the difficulties which students encountered. Inadequate funding for staff indicates the low priority of Native education in the government's budget, and in the Euro-Canadians' concerns.

Memories of the lunch which followed morning classes were little better than those of the breakfast mush.

> They used to put potatoes, turnips, carrots, chunks of meat, cabbage, everything all in one pot and boil the hell out of it. By the time they were ready to serve it, you couldn't even see a little chunk of potato; it was all like a chowder. And that we had for lunch every day . . . .
>
> Fridays: I don't know where they used to go. Up Squilax somewhere I guess, Adams River and they'd get barrels and barrels of that spawned sockeye. They'd put them in barrels of salt and that was what they cooked in great big pans. Then, [they'd] mash it . . . and they'd blob it in our plate and that was what we ate on Fridays: salty fish, always that blue milk. (SOPHIE: 10)

Following lunch, the hard work of the day began. Accompanying the religious people's mission to Christianize was the government's goal to "civilize" the Native people. The program for civilization included teaching students the skills required for farming, gardening, sewing, cooking, and cleaning. The result was beneficial to the residential school in two ways: government requirements were met, and the work necessary for maintaining the school was accomplished. In some years, the operation of the school actually showed a profit, and sums of money were sent to Provincial House in Vancouver. Leo, who several times made reference to his hunger at the school, shared this information:

> We used to collect 300, 350 eggs a day from the chickens . . . . Now we got eggs every second Thursday, one egg apiece . . . . They must have sold the eggs. (31)

Father O'Grady, in a 1954 report on K.I.R.S., wrote that: "The finances are sound and a large surplus is sent annually to the Province" (*Acts of Visitation, 1943-1966: 29*).

The training in agriculture for the males and in household skills for the females was expected to create white people with brown skins: people who would meld into the larger European dominated society. Memories of chores were mentioned by all those interviewed, frequently in greater detail than memories of academic work. Not only did the work occupy considerably more time each day, it also occupied a greater portion of the students' consciousness about their lives. The females' chores were clearly sexually defined. "The afternoon is spent in the kitchen or the sewing room," reported one student who attended in the late thirties. Martha, who attended earlier, recalls:

> I was mostly put in the dairy and in the sewing room but there were a lot of other chores that each of us had . . . . We had to rotate our chores . . . . [In the sewing room], what we were doing was mostly patching clothes and there was some things we had to make like the underwear. (2)

Over the years the amount of sewing done varied. One student described clothing made by cutting up army surplus uniforms and sewing them into tunics. In later years, most of the sewing was confined to patching.

Through rotation of the jobs, students experienced all aspects of housekeeping in order that they become prepared for keeping their prospective homes in good European fashion. The contrast between the homes where the students' families lived and the residence buildings has already been mentioned. For many of those students who attended before mid-century, knowing how to wash and wax a floor was hardly appropriate preparation for life in a house with a dirt floor. Rather the skills learned were intended to prompt students' dissatisfaction with their parents' way of life. Although no one could argue with the importance of developing better housing for some Native people of the area, the method of creating family disharmony and individual confusion about the inherent value of a waxed floor was another tactic in the culturally destructive plans of the residential school authorities. Although those in control may have had little knowledge of Native homes, always the European way was presented as the right and only way to live. Any other way of life was unworthy of discussion and to be despised.

When not occupied in the sewing room or in cleaning, the girls were on duty in the kitchen. Kitchen chores were described as follows:

> When you get into the kitchen, the cook assigned you. Some of them would be the cook's helper, some the pots and pans, and

some the bowls and utensils. One was for the pantry: you sliced the bread and made sure you made enough for the meal and lunch in the afternoon. Then she would assign two girls to the dairy where they churned the butter and made it into pounds. (SOPHIE: 1)

Surprisingly, the cleaning duties were shared by both the boys and the girls. They did, of course, remain segregated, with the girls on one side of the building cleaning their quarters and the boys on the other side cleaning theirs. Teams were assigned to the various areas.

> We had a change of office every month. Mother Superior would come down in an evening and . . . she would read out names of who is going to work in the playroom . . . cleaning the recreation room, the public bathrooms . . . . There was a group assigned to the chapel . . . . A group would go to the second floor—that's the classrooms, superiors' community. The halls had to be shined all the time. Then there was another group went upstairs to the dorm . . . . And then there was a group assigned to the laundry. (SOPHIE: 1)

Charlie reported similiar duties.

> We gradually got introduced to chores . . . . A clean-up team would be composed of some seniors, some intermediates and some juniors . . . which was a good way . . . . At first maybe they were easy on us: we did the dusting. It was a lot similar to how I learned things at home which was good.
>
> We had the bathrooms to do. My job as a little one was to flush all the toilets or to pick up the big things so that the sweeper could sweep . . . . But I gradually got to know what the others were doing . . . we worked as a team . . . . There was enough time to get to know one another. I believe the term was one month at a time and then a new list was given. (7)

The camaraderie which developed within the groups provided a welcome respite from the cultural attacks. As Native children working together, they could revert to traditional ways of dividing the labour in what may have approached the familial way: the older students acting in the role of parents expecting the younger ones to help as they could and gradually to become aware of the more complex tasks to be done. In all likelihood, the reasons for the students' comfort with their work went unrecognized by the supervisors. It is possible that the relative harmony with which cleaning was done was viewed by those in charge as a confirmation that this kind of work was most suitable for the Native students. Through a lack of understanding, the European overseers apparently failed to appreciate that this work provided an opportunity for the expression of the traditional division of labour. A Native graduate of K.I.R.S. who became a supervisor in the school found her approaches to chore supervision different from those of the nuns who had guided her:

> . . . I found too if you treat them good and kind of make them like yourself, that you're not up there and they're down there, that they're easier to get along with and you could get more out of them . . . . I worked with them a lot. I just didn't say, 'You go in there and scrub the kitchen floor.' I got down and I worked with them. (JOSEPHINE: 7)

She attributed this ability to her mother's guidance:

> I spent the first ten years with my mother . . . . I think she was my best teacher . . . . When we weeded, my mum weeded with us, too. I remember her crawling beside us . . . . (JOSEPHINE: 7)

Throughout her years of doing school chores, she remembered most clearly the work she had done with her mother. Cleaning time occupied a considerable portion of the day and, because it was a time when students could interact with one another to a certain extent and when supervision was of necessity less rigorous, it was considered more relaxing than class time or prayer time.

While the girls were cooking and sewing, the boys gardened and farmed. One man had this to say:

> Oh, we learned a little about farming too. Not anything about fertilizer. They never explained to us why they do things. They just told us how to do it, you know, like harrowing, plowing and seeding and planting potatoes . . . . When I got older, my last year or two, I used to do a lot of planting and irrigating in the garden.
>
> They had huge gardens. And they had a planter where you put the seed in and you just follow in a straight line . . . .
>
> And they learn a little bit about dairy, but we never learned anything about planning of anything or the financing or accounting or anything like that. (LEO: 14)

The last comment is coming from the perspective of a man who now understands considerably more about European business style than he did as a child. He recognizes now that the boys were being trained not to run a successful business as farmers, but simply to grow enough food to support their families and to provide a labour pool for neighbouring farms and ranches. Even as assimilation was stated as the goal of education for Native people, the assimilation was to take place under conditions which would cause no threat to the surrounding business and farming community. The notion of control by the cultural invaders in the guise of church and state, was the most powerful determinant of educational policy. The senior boys rose early to care for the livestock.

> The senior boys used to get up . . . in the morning—those that go to the barn and milk the cows, feed the chickens, pigs—5:30 in the morning. You know, work over there an hour and a half. And then you'd come back and go to church for another pretty near an hour and then you'd have breakfast. (LEO: 19)

Charlie, who attended K.I.R.S. ten years later, reports that his work included the following:

> Dairy cattle, beef cattle, chickens, turkeys, horses, going haying . . . . For a little while, we had pigeons, bees. Most of us made the stations working through all of those places so we knew when it was our turn for planting . . . . We'd have a calendar and we'd mark off the date when we planted, harvested and how to test when they were ripe.
>
> Not too many of us used the apprenticeship. I suppose the skills were transferable. (15)

Although this person did not use the farming skills which he learned at school, some did find the skills useful. Some of the boys also got involved with carpentry and shoe repair. These skills were taught as part of the technical school. Those who were selected to attend these classes avoided some of the chore detail so they were pleased to be selected to go.

> If you got into tech, it's nice and warm in the winter. And you learn how to do a bit of carpentry, the basic stuff, make joints and mortise . . . .
>
> One year, I was mending shoes. They had a lathe there and a couple of those shoelaps. They had great big pieces of real thick leather. We used to carve out soles and a heel . . . tack it on and

> then you polish it. And running shoes, we used to sew thin black
> leather or patches . . . . (LEO: 14)

With their newly acquired carpentry skills, the boys were put to
work maintaining the existing buildings, constructing a huge
pig-pen and installing a floor and ceiling in the new gymnasium.

> . . . the boys put in the flooring, finished flooring . . . . They used
> flat-head nails and they nailed it on the tongue so that the nail
> head never showed. And we went over it after we finished. You
> couldn't see a hammer mark . . . . And we put in the donna conna
> ceiling. We had to have high scaffolds, measure it out. We done
> that ourselves. So we learned a little. (LEO: 14)

This person eventually used his carpentry skills in building his
own houses.

The work done by the children was considered of prime
importance by government officials. As late as 1954, the Department of Indian Affairs Annual Report's description of the
curriculum proudly listed the acquisition of these work-related
skills as a part of the course of studies for the majority of Native
children, particularly those " . . . in less advanced areas" *(Dept.
of Citizenship and Immigration, 1956: 51).*

For the church, the inculcation of Catholic values was of
paramount importance. At the bottom of the list of priorities
for both parties was an introduction to basic reading, writing
and arithmetic. The cultural invasion was clearly acknowledged,
detailed and documented. European ways are Canadian ways
and Native people must comply with these expectations. One
school official made this comment during the 1950s:

> The problem of Indian education is not primarily one of giving
> the Indian children the same schooling as all our other children.
> It is a problem of changing the persevering Indian community into
> a Canadian community. Then the Indian child cannot help but
> grow up in a Canadian culture and then the ordinary Canadian
> school will meet their educational needs. (MULVIHILL, 1957: TAPE
> 130-2)

The final part of the school day included an hour of study,
supper, clean-up, some highly structured and closely supervised
recreation time, more prayers, and then bed. Night time found
the children cold, lonely and frequently afraid. "At the Indian
school, you only had one [blanket] no matter how cold it was"

(Linda: 21). The loneliness came with sleeping alone in a bed: many children had been accustomed to sleeping with siblings at home. The fear came with the unknown behind a closed door or with the nightly visits of the watchman.

> We were not allowed to sleep with each other and they were very strict about that. We were not allowed to talk to each other . . . . And at night, the watchman would come around and we were very, very scared of him. We often thought he was wicked and ready to get us. I don't know where we got that idea from. (NANCY: 21)

The fear and loneliness often were manifested in bed-wetting. One person estimated that 25% of the boys wet their beds. A student who left in 1960 remembered her bed-wetting.

> I never did do that when I was home. The first night . . . when I peed the bed, I was so ashamed . . . . I was just filthy dirty. And I couldn't believe that I done it, you know. This is incredible. I never wet the bed at home. Why am I doing it now? And I asked a thousand questions. (LINDA: 14)

Always bedtime was the loneliest part of the day. The children longed for their parents, the warmth of the family bed and the sense of security which they had known.

EXTRACURRICULAR ACTIVITIES

With the late 1940s, numerous changes were made in the school. As well as the introduction of high school, extracurricular activities such as competitive dancing, a brass band and sports took on greater importance. Gradually chore time was reduced as time for these other occupations assumed significance. It is possible that the presentation of Native students performing in public was seen as a positive public relations move by the school's administration as Gresko *(1986: 96)* has claimed about an earlier school. Work was in progress on revisions to the Indian Act, and both the politicians and the school officials were conscious of the fact that the schools which were meant to make Indians disappear had not been successful.

Some students found their successes in various fields rewarding. One student commented that the K.I.R.S. teams " . . . were the best at everything: soccer, basketball, everything" *(Sam: 1)*. The benefits of being on teams were not confined to winning.

Many people felt that simply getting away from the school was the major attraction of participation.

At the same time, informants were justly proud of their achievements while involved in the various sports. One man described his success at boxing. He qualified to fight in the Buckskin Gloves tournament three years running. The ultimate tournament of the year, it required that boys place in the six or seven prior tournaments held throughout the region. Only the top four or five boxers from each region were selected and qualifying to box at even the smaller meets was no mean feat.

> The only outside activity was sports. In order to go and compete anywhere outside, you had to beat out 200 other people. Maybe that's why you were the best out there. Even in boxing you had sixty or seventy other people to beat out each year. So you weren't sparring, you were boxing. (SAM: 8)

Neil, who left the school in 1960, spoke highly of the school largely as a result of his association with team sports. He too felt a keen sense of competition.

> If you stubbed your toe, they just put someone else on. So you had to give 100% . . . . You had to work hard to make the team . . . .
> We got to play for the teams in town. That was what was really enjoyable about this school. The intermediate teams in town drafted students from this school to play. We even got to stay at the coach's house on the weekends. (51)

The fostering of a sense of competition may have held some implications for the control of the students if the divide and rule philosophy was felt to be beneficial by the disciplinarians. Traditionally, Shuswap communities have existed through families cooperating with one another. One person who was very successful in sports found his relationship with his less successful brothers noticeably strained. As a result of the competition fostered between them at school, they have never been close.

The administration's recognition that the school's public image was enhanced through the children's success in competition also played a role in the development of competitive dance groups in the school. Seen by many students as the way to provide variety in their lives, especially with travel to competitions, dancers also recognized the special benefits available to them.

> The only reason why I stayed in the dance group was because you got privileges . . . . Sometimes on Sunday, you didn't have to get up for early Mass. Then you sometimes got extra goodies that other kids didn't get . . . .
>
> I really enjoyed myself when we went to Revelstoke on the train. I thought that was pretty neat . . . . My mum had bought me this really nice hat and dress outfit. (LINDA: 18)

Another student hoped that joining the dance group would help her stay out of trouble.

> I said, 'Well, if I have to stay here, I might as well get something out of this place.' So I decided to join their dancing group . . . . They let me join; I don't know why. You know, I didn't even know if they would take me after running away. (ALICE: 6)

Membership in the dance group was viewed as a prestigious position. Although the training was rigorous, many girls enjoyed the opportunity to feel good about themselves and enjoyed the admiration of outsiders. It is notable that although the dance group performed dances from many European countries such as the four and eight hand reel, Irish jigs and the Swedish masquerade, no Shuswap dances were performed. Even to the final days of the school, the Native culture was not recognized as a legitimate one, worthy of recognition. Although the drum and bugle band wore fake headdresses, and students were eventually permitted to 'Indian dance' for fun, activities generally continued to be fashioned on the European model.

Not all was pleasant for the girls who decided to become dancers. One long-standing member of the group had some particularly bitter memories.

> . . . my toenails are permanently damaged from [having] to stand on your toes. If you didn't stand on your toes, you were whacked with a . . . shillelagh and she'd whack you damn hard on your legs . . . .
>
> The first few times you really tried because you found out that things were a lot better if you were a dancer . . . . You went places too, so that made you want to get out of that school . . . .
>
> But then after a while, it's not fun anymore: it's a chore because you're never any good . . . . They never swore at you but they called you dumb and stupid . . . and so then the fun was out of it. And after a while you kind of didn't want to do it but . . . they

> didn't want to retrain somebody so they'd keep making you do it
> . . . .
>
> I remember the first time I ever got whacked. I stood there and
> thought, 'Well, I'm going to defy this woman' . . . . I just glared at
> her and she gave me another one and I kind of glared. But I wasn't
> glaring too hard 'cause it hurted and the next time she whacked
> me, I really broke down and howled. (LINDA: 17-18)

Even the prizes began to lose their meaning for Linda.

> You won prizes and wondered why the hell you even bothered to
> go because when you got back it was still the same way. (18)

Anne, who observed the dance training, also remembers the
stick.

> If you were dancing, she'd come up and she'd hit you on the legs,
> 'Lift them legs up!' Geez them poor girls would be just a . . . you
> know. They learned those Scottish jigs, the different types of dances
> from the different parts of the world. But the girls really won a lot
> of medals for it so it was good encouragement for them. (2)

While offering some encouragement to the girls, the main
purpose of the dance groups was as a show-piece to be displayed
in public for the school's prestige and to create public support.
The relevance of the dances to the students' lives and the
long-term benefits of the rather savage training are highly
questionable. With no connection to the Shuswap culture, they
appear to be merely someone's idea of what would be good for
'them', the Native children of K.I.R.S.

Before the 50s, a rare few deemed to have exceptional academic ability participated in semi-private dialogic meetings with
stimulating instructors. For those students, the time was a
welcome relief from the impersonal atmosphere of much of the
rest of the day. Some of the lessons dealt with a more philosphi-
cal view of both religion and the academic subjects.

> Some priests here would call a few of us into a dialogue of life
> . . . . They called us in a room and they would just give us the
> freedom to explore different things of life and tie some things
> together . . . .
>
> Another one . . . used to take some of us to have discussions
> about history and almost philosophical areas . . . . His get-togeth-
> ers with us were much like a university seminar. And he'd just

challenge us . . . he would give us time, 'You think of that, close your eyes, extend . . . .' He would say, 'There is a university. There are thousands of books on this. Your mind can keep on going . . . .'

They taught me more about looking at things than the classroom 'cause the classroom was mundane . . . . These were idea things and he respected our ideas, no matter how small they were. (CHARLIE: 16)

The group described met during the forties and consisted of five or six boys out of a school population of 300 or 350. Although these lessons were highly stimulating for those few, many of whom went on to become chiefs and leaders, they were not considered appropriate or wise for the vast majority of children. This kind of careful selection and enrichment for a chosen few is typical of the hierarchical system so much a part of all aspects of European society including the organized Church. It appears to have been an attempt to induct these particular children into the belief system that a special few are entitled to privileges unfit for the general population.

The meetings also provided opportunity for the children involved to experience a setting more like their home environment and to reinforce the Shuswap way of relating to children respectfully. Another notable aspect of this person's comment is " . . . He gave us time." In recent studies of Native learning styles, the amount of time between asking a question and expecting an answer has proven very significant. Many Native students, like many non-Native students, respond with much more regularity and depth when adequate time for thought is allowed. If this notion had been applied in the regular classroom, the success rate of students at the secondary level might have been affected.

Other happy memories center on general recreation time, special holidays and changes for the better.

It wasn't all bad. We had a lot of fun. We looked forward to the picnics, Christmas . . . . We stayed here for Christmas so we used to have little concerts . . . it made us feel good . . . . It was just a real treat to have a bought doll. I got one . . . . Every one of the kids had a bought gift for the first time in our whole life. That was the highlight of my school days.

And then they began buying us beads. We were able to string beads and make little beaded things . . . . We had a radio for the

> playroom . . . . Then the priest allowed us to have dances—just
> girls, no boys . . . . Friday night . . . . We were allowed to wear
> clothes from home . . . . We began to get nicer food. (SOPHIE: 4)

All these changes in the late forties were attributed to a new
principal arriving at the school. A person who attended near the
turn of the century fondly remembered a picnic.

> Gee, one time, the sister and that man that looks after them, we
> went up straight over the mountain. We got some lunch. After we
> got over, way down there's a creek . . . we picnic (they call them
> picnic). (CECILIA: 6)

The opportunity to be in an environment more like home,
particularly like the fondly remembered summer camps, must
have felt good to this little girl. Alice, who attended much later
during the sixties, reminisced about her recreation time.

> . . . in the rec room . . . they used to have a radio there. We used
> to listen to the songs . . . . Elvis Presley . . . . I used to like his songs
> . . . . I don't know how I started learning to dance . . . . This one
> supervisor we had, she said, 'Do you know what? I wished I was a
> good dancer.' She was an Indian lady that they hired . . . . I said,
> 'I think I know how to dance.' . . . so she got her record player
> and she put a record on and I and her started to dance . . . . All
> the other little girls used to watch . . . . Then I started teaching
> them how to dance and after that everybody danced . . . .
>
> We played baseball and sometimes . . . we'd sit around and
> we'd make up stories . . . . 'Boy, if I was rich, I would do this and
> that, you know.' (8)

The presence of a Native person as supervisor, while not changing the system, did make a difference to some aspects of the
children's daily lives. With her, the children would be reminded
of home and would probably have an opportunity for reinforce-
ment of some cultural patterns. This student felt comfortable
enough with a Native supervisor to take a leadership role at
recreation time. She also commented on her fantasies of being
rich.

> I don't know how we were exposed to richness and happiness . . . .
> When we got to intermediate, it was a little harder. 'Cause then
> some of the kids there were a little richer . . . . You get to wear
> your own clothes . . . you're allowed to fix your hair . . . . If you

were poor, you didn't have anything nice . . . . It was a hard time because of the peer pressure. (ALICE: 8)

Peer pressure can be particularly devastating when children are exposed to it twenty-four hours a day. For children who are with their families the pressure time may be limited to school hours. In the residential school, there was no escape. In this case, as with the dancing group, the happy times are tainted with some painful memories.

Alice spoke negatively of recreation time. A particular priest was the cause of her concern.

> That one priest he was kind of odd . . . . I was kind of scared of him, I guess . . . . We were at the movie there one Friday night. He went and he sat with the little girls. I was kind of watching and I said, 'Gee, it must be nice to have a friend.' . . . . Anyway, I ended up beside him . . . and all of a sudden he started to feel my legs . . . . I was getting really uncomfortable and he started trying to put his hands in my pants . . . . And I just got up and I moved right away but I never thought to tell anybody. (9)

A number of people mentioned sexual overtures made to them during their time at school. This priest also was known to spend extensive time around the little girls when they played outside. His oppression of people went beyond the racial to the sexual.

In a much lighter vein, one student recollected an incident connected to Indian dancing at the school. This was the only reference to Indian dancing made by the informants I interviewed. Of significance is that, by this time in the late fifties, religious and political pressures had exerted enough influence that people in power were confident that Native culture was rapidly disappearing. For this reason, some dancing could be allowed without jeopardizing the intent of bringing Native people into mainstream European-influenced society. As a new student at the school, this teenager was challenged by other students to show her Indianness. In response to the nun's inquiry as to who knew how to Indian dance,

> . . . one of those two hollered out, 'Anne knows how to Indian dance' and I didn't . . . . So Sister says, 'O.K. get up there and dance.' And I thought, 'Oh my God. I don't know what the heck I'm doing.' And I thought the only person that's going to know the mistake . . . are the girls themselves because they're Indian.

> Sister ain't going to know so she ain't going to hit me on the legs
> . . . . I got up there and just did a war whoop and dance, just really
> faked it. (ANNE: 2)

With that performance, the new girl passed the test put to her and was accepted by them.

Most noteworthy about the extracurricular activities is that they provided a respite from the regimented day. They also provided an opportunity for some students to grow in confidence and self-esteem. While still predominantly denying the existence of the Native culture, they did serve in some cases as a successful foundation on which the students could build. At the least, the recreational activities gave students a chance to relax, to know one another, to remember and practice some culturally related behaviours and to dream a little of what might be.

DISCIPLINE

Discipline in the Kamloops Indian Residential School was severe. Based perhaps on the old saying 'Spare the rod and spoil the child', punishment was a topic raised repeatedly by informants. The strap was mentioned most frequently, but other forms of punishment including public humiliation, head shaving and bread and water diets were also reported. Cecilia, the oldest person interviewed, recollected:

> Some people got punished; they got to lay down on the floor. Just
> pure bread and water to eat, laying on the floor . . . oh, I don't
> know how many days. (2)

Martha brought to mind these scenes.

> I was punished quite a bit because I spoke my language . . . . I was
> put in a corner and punished and sometimes, I was just given
> bread and water . . . . Or they'd try to embarrass us and they'd put
> us in front of the whole class. (6)

Public humiliation was one of the worst forms of punishment for the children. Traditionally other people laughing at a person served as a strong social control. James Teit, in his extensive anthropological study of the Shuswap, recounts lists of taboo behaviours almost all of which include the warnings that those who do such things will be laughed at or gossiped about.

Frequently, to add insult to injury the strap was given publicly.

> ... if we got caught, we really got punished and if that didn't work, we got sent to the principal's office. And that was lashes we got there, in front of the whole school: real humiliation. (SOPHIE: 3)

Another student who attended in the sixties recalled:

> I got in trouble for chewing gum .... It was such a minor, minor thing in my view. But I was taken into the playroom .... She was a lay person. She took down my pants right in front of everybody .... Can't remember whether she used her hand to spank me or whether she used a ruler or a strap ... but I remember being punished. (NANCY: 16)

Another student remembered the worst strapping she received because of its injustice.

> One time, we were issued these barrettes .... You only got one a year .... One of the intermediates had lost hers so she said, 'Can you lend it to me until right after the check?' .... It was the very time that sister noticed I didn't have it on .... I got the strap for that .... I didn't want to tell on the girl either so I got punished. (JOSEPHINE: 4)

She remembers there were a " ... lot of strappings going on .... They took your pants down and they lean you over a bench in front of everybody"(16). Again public humiliation was combined with corporal punishment. Perhaps the punishers understood enough of Shuswap culture to know that public humiliation was the worst form of punishment or perhaps a lack of awareness caused them to punish children doubly. In either case, the punishments used, although efficient, appear inhuman in retrospect.

Bedwetters were also punished severely.

> When I was a junior, I used to wet the bed—whipped us for that, too. He had a scheme; he tried to stop people from wetting the bed .... First of all he tried to get us up a couple of times at night .... For a lot of us it didn't work so he thought he'd do it the hard way, give them whippings .... He finally quit doing it. That was on your bare [bottom] too. (LEO: 15)

Other children remembered having their wet sheets put over

their heads and then being spanked. One admitted, "I don't remember that part or I don't want to remember" *(Sophie: 16)*. Such memories were too painful to live with and were repressed. A man recalled that the little boys had to wash their sheets in the river and that his daughter had been locked in a cupboard for continual wetting of her bed *(Field notes)*. Several others mentioned washing their own sheets every day. Bedwetting, so frequently a manifestation of children who are upset in some way, was a sure sign that life was very stressful for many children at K.I.R.S.

Head shaving was another form of punishment actually considered more severe than strapping, perhaps because of the traditional associations already mentioned. The initial haircut was punishment enough. Shaving was worse.

> As a little girl, my hair was really long and curly . . . my hair was down to my hips . . . . Sister cut it; she kept cutting it till she shaved my hair 'cause she thought I was curling my hair . . . . It was very evil for us to have curly hair. Everything we did was evil. (MARTHA: 12)

A runaway in the early 60s, Alice retraced these painful steps:

> When I got back to the school, because I ran away, they were going to give me punishment. So instead of strapping me, they said, 'You got to kneel down on the floor, in front of everybody and tell them you're sorry you ran away . . . .' Because I ran away, they said they were going to give me a real short hair cut for punishment. So my hair was cut really short, almost like a boy's. (6)

By this time, the disciplinarians must have recognized that public mortification was the worst form of chastisement for the children and that head shaving was effective in that it created long-term easily recognized disgrace.

Other incidental disciplinary action was also mentioned. One brother who looked after the first aid post provided this gruesome treatment to a child who had scratched the sore on top of his head.

> He had a pitcher there and he used to always have castor oil in it. When he got mad at somebody . . . he'd take that castor oil and grab him by the hair and fill his mouth up . . . . I must have been about 7 or 8 years old then. He pulled my head back and he filled my mouth with castor oil and pretty near made me gag. Then he kept my head back till I swallowed it. (LEO: 16)

This treatment was nothing short of cruel and unusual punishment inflicted by a short-tempered person. Whether the action was common is not known, but the presence of the jug suggests perhaps it was. Another episode of castigation involved a little boy who was hungry.

> One thing that sticks in my mind was the one little guy . . . . Poor little thing, I guess he was so hungry, he used to go down to the river bank and pick those thorn berries . . . . One day he filled all his little pockets . . . and the darn principal, he was so mean. He grabbed that little boy and turned him upside-down by his legs and shook him. Berries went all over the floor. The little boy stood there crying. All these humiliating things that they did to us. (SOPHIE: 3)

Although the inflictions suffered by the students were numerous, little could be done about them. Until the fifties, students were in residence eleven months of the year. Letters written home were always censored. Leo reported the following:

> They censored all our letters. If you made a complaint . . . they would make a big speech—if we complained about food in a letter. There wasn't very many that complained . . . 'cause we knew it wouldn't get out anyway. (12)

Another person wrote to her grandmother to ask if she could live with her instead of staying at the school.

> I never did ever get an answer from her . . . . I didn't know that the nuns never sent the letter 'cause they read [it] . . . . They'd censor your letters and so they never bothered sending my letter. (LINDA: 15)

Punishment of all sorts was an integral part of the work of the children's keepers. Children were to learn to be obedient, to abandon their cultures and to comply with regulations. Perceived lack of co-operation was dealt with quickly. One could assume that under the circumstances—of many children and few staff—these measures were expedient. The appropriateness of the castigations and the long term effects are more questionable. In retrospect, the punishments seem unnecessarily severe.

FAMILY VISITS AND SUMMER HOLIDAYS

Family visits and summer holidays created a myriad of complex feelings for the children at K.I.R.S. Although remembered with mixed feelings, contact with family provided some continuity and support for the students and left them with the feeling that while school might feel inescapable, outside its walls, Shuswap life carried on. Ultimately this interaction may be seen as positive; at the time, the children felt torn. During the interviews, many people expressed common feelings; for others, the feelings were specific to their lives. For those whose families saw value in adaptation to some of the European ways, less disruption of family relationships occurred. Throughout the school's existence, children whose parents could not or did not confide in them about the purpose of school were the most affected by its invasive nature.

A commonly mentioned reaction to parents was one of anger and a feeling of rejection on being sent to the school. For these children, family visits tended to reinforce the confusions.

> We were there from August; we only had one month's summer holiday and that was July . . . . We never even went home for Christmas and we were allowed parent visits only about once a month . . . .
>
> In time they come; you got used to it, [the school] . . . . You were torn in-between . . . . I know I blamed my parents for putting me there because I felt they didn't want me. And I blamed the sisters and the fathers that they were trying to take something away from me . . . . I felt I was beginning to have hate . . . . I was beginning to have resentment against my mother and my dad because I felt . . . that they didn't love me, that they just put me in there and threw me to the wolves. (MARTHA: 14)

Martha recalled a tremendous feeling of self-control when her mother visited.

> I remember they came once in the fall and just for a little while . . . . They came in the truck and I went with them in the truck just a little ways. We sat and we talked and it felt really different . . . . There are no tears or anything because I understood what is going to happen for a few years. But I think if I was younger I might have been clawing her and scratching her. But I'm a young lady, eh, and I know why. It was nice she came. (6)

The final comment demonstrates the importance of the mother's visit for this person despite her internal ambivalence.

View of the Kamloops Indian Residential School from the south side.

Interior of classroom at KIRS.

KIRS boys put on gymnastic display.

Dormitory in KIRS in 1930s or 1940s.

Chapel at KIRS.

Sewing classes at KIRS in the 1930s.

Boys from KIRS attending movie at the Capital Theatre, Kamloops, c. 1940s.

Staff, pupils and parents at KIRS for Easter communion.

Although some of the feelings of disappointment may be attributed to children's unrealistic expectations of family visits, just below the surface were feelings that somehow the visit would save them from the oppressive system, that miraculously they would be able to go home and be a part of the family again. Such wistful feelings may be common to some adults seeking a lost childhood, but healthy confident children might look forward to approaching years. The reactions reinforce the notion that school was an unhappy place to be, even for those who knew why they were there.

In contrast, Neil, who attended in the 1960s, found that the regular bi-weekly visits of a mentor-uncle were of great significance to his positive experiences at the school. This uncle who took the student away from the school during his visits, offered advice and encouragement, suggesting ways to make the most of his school experience. The uncle's never-failing interest, particularly in the student's participation in team sports, was a great support for the student and also helped him develop a keen sense of competition which has served him well.

For some people whose parents were far away or busy with a large family at home, visits were impossible.

> Some kids had parents that came all the time but . . . where we live way up here . . . you had to catch the train . . . . I think once [when] we were at the school they travelled way down to go to work in the tomato fields; they travelled down with their horse and wagon. And money was hard to come by so we didn't get anything. We never come home at Christmas. A lot of children did but, as I grew older, I thought that was just it because there we had the whole school and everything was just relaxed. (JOSEPHINE: 3)

Over time, this student grew accustomed to school, and accustomed to seeing little of her parents during the school year. Her distance from the family's way of life also grew.

Although some parents took children away from the school during their visits, many described rather stiff meetings in the school parlour with the principal frequently hovering nearby. These visits were one of the few occasions that siblings of different ages and sex were permitted to be together.

> I can't remember what holiday it was, but my parents came to visit . . . . I was really happy to see them. I wanted to go home right

> away but my mum . . . said that I couldn't go home. It was really
> hard to see them leave us . . . .
>
> We met in this one room they called the parlour and there
> was a few benches in the room . . . . The priest would come
> around to the door once in a while and the principal would say
> hello . . . .
>
> I didn't know why I had to stay, why they couldn't say I could
> go home with them because I thought, 'Well, they're my mum and
> dad. They used to decide whether I could go home with them or
> not.' Before I went there, they used to leave us with sitters and
> they'd come and pick us up. I couldn't understand why they
> couldn't just say, 'O.K. let's go home.' (ALICE: 3)

While the connections made between family members during
these visits were clearly important in maintaining a kind of
family unity and a sense of culture of origin, the pain at being
separated again was excruciating. In the plan to have students
become a part of Euro-Canadian culture, visits were somewhat
of a detriment in that they reminded the child who he was and
who his family was. In the maintenance of a sense of being
Indian, being part of a family, they were integral.

Holidays raised similar quandaries in the students' minds.
Adjustment periods were common when students arrived
home. Linda remembered her siblings' return.

> [They] would come home from that school and they weren't
> running around and being themselves. They were quiet and some-
> times just sat for hours . . . . My younger brother and I were just
> [thinking], 'Oh, these guys are really bloopers: they just sit and do
> nothing.'
>
> Mum would say, 'You kids, get out there and feed the chickens,'
> and John or Rosie would say, 'That's not my job' . . . .
>
> By then, they were defying Mum . . . . They got so they had to
> get lickings to get them to go do things. (8)

For the whole family, adjustments were necessary. The children
felt out of place and had begun to assume behaviours common
to residential school. Rather than recognizing that duties were
shared by the family, they began to defy parents and expect
punishment as a means of enforcing rules.

Language was another area of concern. For some the transition back to their native language was smooth. As time went on,
more of the parents spoke only English in response to their own

training at the residential school—training which convinced them that their language had no place in Euro-Canadian society—and as a result of increasing involvement with English speakers both Native and non-Native.

> When I learned my Shuswap, we lived as a total family unit. Previous to 1938, there was not much moving about outside of the reserve area . . . . When I came to school . . . . I can see now my father began branching out working away from home; my grandfather went farther away from home . . . . The Shuswap language continued to be spoken whenever they [the family] got together but as we gained more knowledge of the English and because of ranching out, [work] in logging camps, they moved gradually to speak more English. And then when we all came home, I could see the switch into English as we started to move through the years . . . .
>
> They would slip into Shuswap whenever an elder would come who had not left the reserve and they would just flick back and forth in that way . . . . That happened in our family and I think that happened in a large number of other families. (CHARLIE: 5)

This quotation summarizes very clearly the erosion of the language which occurred in the Kamloops area. By the last few years of the school's operation, students coming to school almost all had prior knowledge of English and in some cases had never learned their own language. Those who had suffered for speaking Native languages wanted to help their children avoid similar treatment.

For some students going home just felt good.

> We were poor, eh, and I don't know why going home was so good. Because—love is what covers it all. And then you're free to talk and you're just right back and it's all open, open door again . . . . For the first few days, we were speaking English and then after a while we started mixing it. And then by end of summer we were speaking Shuswap again. (MARY: 14)

Leo had similar feelings. He acknowledged that although . . .

> . . . it wasn't as clean . . . . I was happier at home . . . . I know I get lots to eat and I get a bit of free time . . . . I could play. I had to work sometimes making hay, and weeding the garden but I was just as happy to be home. When we had our chores done, we could roam the country. Do as we wish. (16)

The plentiful food supply of summer and the contrast to the oppressive system of the school may have coloured these people's memories. At the same time, the memories serve to emphasize the authoritarian nature of school. When children prefer making hay and weeding gardens to school life, one must assume that school's tasks are more arduous. In the final analysis, these home visits were very likely integral to maintaining a sense of self, family and culture distinct from the residential school.

For some children in the later years, going home became a time of disappointment. Anticipated with excitement, the reality of a family and a culture being eroded by pressures of an increasingly domineering European influence was not always pleasant.

> Because we were then all through the system, we clung together, you know, like just us kids. And Mum and Dad were kind of out . . . . By then they'd started drinking. See, when we first started going to that school they never drank . . . . I guess because there was none of us kids at home, they started drinking so when we came home, it was something different. I mean there was booze in the house, there was parties and things started really changing from what we knew of it before . . . . (LINDA: 32-33)

When the parents no longer had their children with them, alcohol could ease their sense of loss. Alice felt a personal sense of shame at her parents' drinking: "I thought, 'Wow, these guys are drunks,' and it was like I didn't have a place anywhere—not at the school and not at home" (6).

Nancy recalled her homecoming as follows:

> Upon arriving home, we would be really excited . . . . and then there would be a drunk Daddy, Mum not feeling so very good and that would bring down the whole excitement. You'd be disappointed but you would be glad to see your parents . . . .
>
> After like a day or so, we would be back into playing outside, looking at the old playgrounds . . . and spending some time with Mum in bed with her telling stories . . . .
>
> I remember as I got older when I went home, I found it hard to speak our language to my parents . . . . I remember stumbling, stumbling, stumbling and the words not coming fluently so I think we were rusty for quite awhile. (18)

Home visits then held two main feelings: a sense of happiness too often accompanied by a growing sense that life had changed irrevocably. This change was not simply the gradual one of children growing older. Consciously or subconsciously, the children recognized that the culture which defined them and their parents was not acceptable to the dominant society around them.

Summers ended and the children returned to school. Bittersweet memories of the last days stand out in one person's mind.

> Before we'd go back to school, we'd go bring the cows in . . . . We'd stay out in the bloody mountains and just thoroughly enjoy ourselves . . . . It would be just about like how it was before but, you know, you'd never ever get back to it because . . . you got a lot of hurts for feelings and you know what's ahead of you. (LINDA: 35)

The impossibility of living as a family on a continual basis and the understanding that life would never be as it was are clearly stated. Mary, who said she actually enjoyed school, remembers her first days back after the holidays.

> I knew I couldn't stay home. I knew that. But the times that really, really gets to the bottom of my soul: the first day back . . . . You're feeling pretty lonesome, suddenly go to bed and in the morning, you wake up and you see this white ceiling. You may as well have a knife and stab me through my heart . . . .
>
> You know where you are and you got to survive and you just cover it over, seal it up for ten months. (14)

Mary's attempt to seal up her real self for ten months in order to survive the oppressive system was one way of protecting her identity as a family member and Shuswap person. With the return to school, the attack on family ways of life was renewed. This time the students knew what the system held for them, but found little security in that knowledge.

One must face the inevitable question of why parents sent their children to the K.I.R.S. For some, an understanding of the importance of reading and writing was paramount. The Oblates did a good job of convincing people that parochial school was the most effective place for learning the catechism. The Department of Indian Affairs included a clause in the Indian Act stating that attendance was mandatory: failure to comply carried fines and imprisonment as penalties. Martha, who attended the school herself and who wanted to keep her children out reported the following:

> With the experience I had as a child, I did not want to see my children being given the abuse I had . . . . When we first sent our children to the public school, we fought the system . . . . The Department of Indian Affairs went as far as saying we'd lose our status . . . . They said we'd have to pay for our children's education. We said we would because we didn't want our children to suffer the way we did . . . .
>
> The Oblates told us we'd go to Hell. They really sort of discriminated against us . . . . They told us that the white man's teaching would corrupt the children's minds. (19-20)

In the face of this opposition, this family finally relented and sent their children to the residential school as day pupils. Other parents recognized the power of the dominant society and hoped that school could ensure an equal position for their children.

> I don't ever remember any of my grandfather or mother telling me about the nature, about the culture of Indians. They never spoke about the Indian culture and I think they already were starting to forget even as old as they were. They seen a white man . . . in a better world so they didn't stress our culture . . . . There was a few things they would teach you. (LEO: 23)

Leo also told extensive stories about details of Shuswap culture, including eating Indian food from the wild. Important to note are his feelings about his parents' thoughts. He received the message that European ways are superior to Shuswap ways. Nancy, who attended years later, reported that her father thought the whites "were the smartest human beings on earth" (6).

Other students interviewed reported more practical reasons for their attendance. Leo, in reference to his foster parents, recounted:

> They send the kids so they don't have to feed them in the winter. You know, these are the facts of life. You can't deny it . . . . Big families didn't have enough to feed some. (7)

Years later, Sam, who transferred into K.I.R.S. after spending some time in public school explained:

> The only reason I was able to go to school in town was because I stayed home with Mum. If they could support you at home, then you could go. (7)

Later when no one was working at home, residential school

became a necessity as his mother found it impossible to provide for the children. In retrospect, Linda, another informant, understood her mother's unspoken reasons.

> It was just what she figured was best for us. Like she wanted us to learn the white man's way so we'd get ahead in the world. And here we thought she hated us. (10)

Many children did not attend. Some came late at the age of nine or ten. Many left early when they became sick and just never returned.

> The priest sends me home. I'm always sick. I don't stay. Go to school every day—ear-ache, sore throat, oh, all kinds of sickness. So the priest send me home. He told me, 'I'll talk to the people to come down for you and they take you home—no use to stay here.' (CECILIA: 1)

Martha, another student, reported:

> The only way I got out was I was very sick. So my father and mother went to Indian Affairs and told them. I had scarlet fever then . . . . I got out . . . and I only had grade three. (16)

Neither of these two ever returned to school. One informant recounted that his parents took him home from school after a sibling was killed in an accident at home. They wanted to have him close to them *(Field notes)*. Some children ran away and were well hidden. Some did not find their names on the list in the fall. One child who sincerely wanted to attend was kept home to do chores for an aging grandmother *(Field notes)*.

Those parents who did send their children did so for one or more reasons. They recognized the importance of literacy, they were respectful of the church's wishes, they believed that European ways were superior, or they found feeding their families difficult because their traditional hunting and food gathering lands were disappearing *(viz. Redford, 1979/80)*. As time went on, more parents kept their children home either to attend the growing number of day schools established on reserves or to go to public school. Others who lived close to the residential school decided to send their children as day pupils when this choice became possible.

CHAPTER 4
THE RESISTANCE

" . . . 'the lads' of this study have adopted and developed to a fine degree in their school counter-culture specific working class themes: resistance; subversion of authority; informal penetration of the weaknesses and fallibilities of the formal; and an independent ability to create diversion and enjoyment."

Paul Willis (1977: 84)

As was the case with Willis' lads in the quote above, Native children also produced counter-cultures in their resistance to the oppressive system which was Kamloops Indian Residential School. People rarely comply fully and easily to the introduction of oppression. Even with the controls already described well in place, the students found time and space to express themselves and to produce a separate culture of their own within the school. Much of this culture was built around opposition to the severity of the rules and regulations guiding the students' daily lives. Another major facet of the resistance was expressed in the development of a sub-culture—one distinct from that being promoted by the religious orders. While it included challenges to the school officials, this culture also took on a life of its own. There were also students who sought refuge within the system as a means of immediate survival but whose actions led to eventual changes within it.

Stealing was common throughout the school. Because hunger was prevalent, food was the main target. It was stolen for immediate personal use, for sharing with smaller children, for barter, and to enhance the scanty meals of the dining room. Those who worked in the kitchen had easy access to food.

> Because we're on that side [the girls' side], you're accessed to the food. [They] usually even take oranges into their friends. If there is some whiney kid, then you can steal some oranges and go and give it to them. Then you got a piece of bread because it's all there.

98

You're the one that slices it and sister doesn't count how many pieces you got. (JOSEPHINE: 21)

The sharing of stolen food resulted in the development of a particular sub-culture. Because stealing became a complex operation, there were often several involved in the act itself as well as guards on look-out and those involved in the distribution of the goods. Martha's account which follows demonstrates the complexity of the arrangements.

In my time, we were always hungry . . . . I seen them bringing in boxes and boxes of apples not too far from the dairy room. So I got these young women and I said, 'How are we going to get some apples?' . . . . So for days and days the girls were scrounging around for strings and my job was to look for spike nails . . . . We tied the strings together and there was an airhole in the root cellar. So we'd have all these girls watching out for us . . . and we'd try to spike apples. That's how we used to get our apples to feed the little ones . . . .

We got caught and we got punished but it took a long time because we supported each other in our crime. (11)

The boys also found their way to the root cellar, sometimes with spears. Although they had access to the barns and all that was produced there, they sometimes resorted to eating cattle food or wild plants and berries in season.

It depends on the time of year. In the fall . . . there were berries and chokecherries and carrots and stuff like that but as . . . [they] went, we started eating grain, bran or wheat. And they would mix this cow feed . . . we used to eat that too and we'd eat mangles even . . . .

When we got higher up, we used to go down to the cellar and steal whenever we could . . . . Now, this time of year [May], you know those rose bushes, they have that berry on them . . . we'd eat that berry. Earlier in the spring when the shoots come out on the rose bush . . . we used to eat that. It's sweet . . . .

We used to eat those things like wild onions and you wouldn't believe it . . . that mustard weed. That's awful. That was toward spring when the cellar was empty. (LEO: 14-20)

Food was uppermost in many students' minds. Several people mentioned gathering berries of all kinds and carrying them with them to eat as snacks. This action was not permitted by the supervisors but as more than one person proudly claimed, 'We never get caught.'

Sophie described how useful her bloomers had been.

> We used to go in the provision room downstairs and there used to be buckets and buckets . . . full of dried prunes, apricots, apples, raisins, nuts that they used to cook for the staff only. And boy, we didn't let them have it all . . . . We'd duck in there if it was open and grab a handful of this and a handful of that, shove it up your bloomer legs. Fill it up and take off down the hall and go into the bathroom and take it all out . . . we'd go around nibbling on that. And then other girls that couldn't steal would barter for it. (1)

The fact that something of a routine developed around this stealing indicates that it was a frequent occurrence. Because of the limited amount of food supplied by the school, the children depended on their stealing and bartering. It became an integral and exciting part of daily life—one in which the children, unless they were caught, could feel some sense of power and control.

Another routine was established by a group of boys who worked in the dairy using their position to institute a complicated process which ensured a more nutritious and tastier breakfast.

> At night, one of those that separated the milk . . . would come along and tap on that window from the outside . . . . He'd have a beer bottle full of cream. I'd take it and put it down in that space in the chaff and leave it till morning . . . . Then, after we clean the horses and feed them . . . . I put that cream in my boot . . . . And then, I'd take it into breakfast and we'd put that on our mush . . . . I was the carrier. We done that and never got caught. (LEO: 21)

At this point, the hunger was refined to a taste for cream. Important to note is the camaraderie created by the common involvement in the crime. One can imagine the feeling of self-satisfaction the boys had as they tasted their ill-gotten gains.

The search for power also had implications for students who served as agents of the supervisors. Some children would tell the authorities about their peers' misdemeanours. Because these informants had to be controlled, those who were misbehaving frequently built in methods for restraining them.

At times students used the threat of informing as blackmail, as Linda shows in the following example.

> We'd crawl along this ditch and get to the apple orchard and sneak apples back . . . [two boys] were stealing apples and we hadn't got to the apple orchard yet. But they were on their way back, so we threatened if they didn't give us any apples, we were going to squeal on them. So they gave us some apples. (7)

This incident took place in the late fifties when an apple orchard was in production at the school. Shortly after, it was levelled and replaced by a new dormitory building. The most amazing aspects of the stealing were its prevalence and the complexities of the various schemes for acquiring and distributing the goods.

Stealing wine was also brought up as a recurring incident in the school. Cecilia recalls:

> Gee, some kids, some boys and girls, they must have steal some wine. That's wine the priest used. They must have steal some [but] they don't get drunk over wine. (2)

Linda, who attended in the 1950s, reported the following incident. She had been assigned to clean up the back of the chapel after the priest said Mass.

> Then this one day, this one boy knocked on the back door. So I opened the door to check what was there and he looked at me and said, 'Oh, where's C____?' and I said, 'She doesn't work here anymore. I do.' So that was that; he went away.
>
> And about the third time, I was back there again and he knocks on the door and says, 'I've got a nickel if you can fill this little jar up.' So I says, 'With what?, Salt water? You got to be crazy.' And he says, 'No, no, not holy water. I want wine.' And I got big eyes, 'No way. Go away.' So that lasted for about, I think, a week I held out.
>
> And then we had a candy store every Sunday morning . . . . Everybody else was going to buy candy and here I am with no money and wanting candy . . . . So that Sunday, the same guy came and knocked on the door. 'Please fill this up,' he said. 'I'll give you a dime.' So I said, 'Okay.' I took the jar and there was three gallons opened so I took a little bit out of each one to fill the thing up and he gave me the dime.
>
> So away he went and . . . . I was really spooky—I mean I was scared. I went out and knelt down and prayed in front of that altar

. . . . 'I'll never, ever do this again. I promise.' I swore up and down I wouldn't . . . . Then nothing seemed to happen to me. I checked myself out; my hair was still there. And I didn't have nits . . . . I never got sick or anything so I thought that was pretty good.

So then he come again . . . . I would sell to them but I would take it out of each jar. And then if it looked like I might have taken too much, I would put a little water in the wine . . . . I never got caught at it neither. I quit praying. I did that for two years. (2-4)

This story indicates the degree to which an individual in the school might be involved in a form of 'organized crime'. The lessons the seller learned were very significant to her: stealing was profitable and one could stall the buyer to achieve a larger profit. Stealing wine that was used by the priest first of all justified prayer but, when immediate retribution failed to materialize, became just business. Not only was the theft accomplished but she also learned to cover her tracks. Additionally, the boys who were paying for the wine were engaged in an interesting process. In both cases, the amount of wine was insignificant. Reportedly it was divided amongst several boys. Again within a repressive situation, the children could gain some sense of self-esteem in repeatedly succeeding at their self-assigned task. The students' awareness of the chinks in the armor of the oppressor provided hope for their survival as individuals with agendas of their own.

Defiance manifested itself in ways other than thievery. Alternating between verbal and non-verbal defiance, one student dealt with the injustices of the system.

That's why the name calling, I used to call the nun [in Shuswap] . . . that's 'dirty behind nun'.

And the thing I remembered when she used to strap me . . . . I knew I was going to get five or ten straps on each hand and I knew it was going to draw blood—but I would remind myself, 'It's not going to hurt. Just so I can make you angry, I'm not going to let you know it hurts . . . ' and I would just stare at her in the face . . . . and I wouldn't even let a drop, a tear come down. God, that used to make her mad. She'd even take me and shake my head and say, 'The devil is in you so strong. How am I going to beat the devil out of you?' She'd put me in a dark place and tell me to stay there. I was a bad example for the rest. (SOPHIE: 2)

With her dignity relatively intact and the nun's frustration leading her to make a display of outrage, Sophie felt she had won the battle. She was not humiliated because she did not cry. Although she was punished, she maintained her control. Other people spoke of maintaining their dignity through silence. Often interpreted as passivity by the more vocal Euro-Canadians, silence, for many Natives, is a sign of strength.

Mary showed her anger first by silencing herself and, in a later incident, in a more dramatic way. Her mother, who had little money, had managed to send her two beautiful new blouses. She was told that she could keep only one and must give the other away.

> She [the nun] did not know or understand anything about home and how hard it was for my mum to get things and I know this. And yet here is a system and so if she says so, that be done. Well, you just numb yourself . . . . You make a choice and you numb yourself to that hurt. (7)

The fact that this person saw herself making an active choice not to speak out about her hurt also gave her a sense of self-esteem. She realized that the nun did not know about her life as she did. In that knowledge, she was stronger than the person causing her pain. She seemed to understand the futility of trying to explain to this foreigner why the blouses were so important.

In another incident, the repercussions for the nun's ignorance were immediate.

> Everybody was getting sick and we all had to take castor oil. So God has ways to get even, too . . . . At home I found out I could not take it . . . . Sister said, 'You're no different than the rest of them.' . . . . She made me take it. It came right back on her apron . . . . It was funny and I pretended I was apologetic and I got cleaned up. (MARY: 8)

This student felt that she had made a verbal effort to present her situation. When it was ignored, she inwardly rejoiced at the outcome. It gave her confidence when she realized she was right: the nun's failure to respond brought its own retribution.

Incidents of this nature were viewed as great jokes on the supervisors. The Indian dancing episode mentioned previously is another example of this kind of resistance to the people in control. All the girls knew that Anne's dance was a mockery.

Because of her fearless performance and the nun's acceptance of it as bona fide Indian dancing, she became an accepted group member with the other students who found her behaviour hilarious *(2)*.

For some students, language was another area for defiance. Again the betrayers had to be watched for, but some students served to educate newcomers about situations where Native languages could be used without fear of reprisal.

> First year, I guess we were, and Leona came and we were all talking Shuswap . . . . She said to us, 'You're never to get caught talking your language . . . . You'll get whipped; you'll really get punished.' . . . So we were careful after that not to be caught speaking . . . . When we were way out there, we'd talk together in our language. (MARY: 8)

Neil, who attended in the fifties, recalled that he found it "tough for about a year. I was kind of careful where I used it" *(1)*. One Chilcotin speaker, Nancy, held defiantly to her language within herself because there were few others in K.I.R.S. who spoke it.

> I remembered trying to remember some words . . . . I was trying to remember one word and that was squirrel and it was so easy . . . . I remember struggling with it all day and trying to remember. And then at night when I went to bed, I kept thinking about it and I thought and thought and then it came up—'dltg.' (16)

Nancy implicitly recognized the importance of maintaining contact with her roots through language. Although she worked alone to remember, she felt a strong need to keep the words in her thinking vocabulary. The time for reunion with other Chilcotin speakers was inevitable. For her, the language never lost its power and influence.

Connecting with the opposite sex was another major preoccupation, particularly with some of the older students. The kitchen presented ideal opportunities for exchanging looks, quick words and sometimes notes as the boys delivered milk, cream, and eggs. Line-ups for meals and time in the chapel were other prime times for exchanges including the oft-mentioned technique of mirror flashing.

> They're not always just hovered over all the time. Like when I worked in the kitchen, those boys came for the garbage. You saw them in church every morning . . . . A lot of them, they had

> mirrors. So if you had a boyfriend in the back you had a little mirror in front of your hymn book . . . . There were notes constantly flying back and forth somehow or another. There were communications. (JOSEPHINE: 16)

In communicating with boys, another complex system was developed again with care to avoid the tattlers and with deliveries made by messengers. One particularly ingenious method of note-passing was devised by a girl who worked in the kitchen: she sliced the crust of bread extra thick, cut a space in the middle, and hid a note there which was delivered to her boyfriend's table. Older teenagers sometimes managed to meet at the river bank. Sophie commented:

> Nature is so strong. You can't help it; you can never destroy nature. Your body grows . . . . I don't care if you cover it up with layers and layers of clothes, it is still doing its thing as a human being. (12)

The resistance to an unnatural control of common human feelings was strong and effective. Despite the school's intensive efforts to completely segregate the sexes, communication occurred.

For the girls, hair curling and using make-up constituted another related form of resistance. These were probably perceived by the school staff as manifestations of the evil influences of white culture. For the children, they were another way of expressing a small amount of control within the authoritarian structure in which they found themselves.

> You were not allowed to put make-up on your face or let alone put a kiss curl in your hair . . . . If you tried, the nun would grab us by the top of the head and drag us under the sink and turn it on full blast . . . many's the time, I got half drownded. (SOPHIE: 2)

Sophie also remembered Sunday afternoon walks with pleasure and a touch of defiance.

> We'd pool our bits of monies together and . . . [two girls] they'd buy a tube of lipstick and rouge and powder and cold cream . . . . On Sunday afternoon when we'd go for a long walk, we would make sure we were way up front where the nun is in the rear. And when we heard her blow the whistle . . . we used to carry a little

> wet cloth with us. We'd wipe that stuff off and then we'd run back
> . . . . I guess we must have looked like a bunch of clowns. (2)

Each small step out of line was an important one in self-defini-
tion. In a society determined by the powers of the priests and
nuns the students' self-produced sub-culture was an even more
important and fundamental aspect of survival.

Some students who found co-operation with the school's
authority palatable under most circumstances, became defiant
in defense of the injustice dealt to the lawbreakers.

> I became a kind of an advocate for some of the people who I
> thought couldn't help themselves. I often became too outspoken
> in helping a person out of a jam. In trying to rationalize why they
> did it, why one was caught with carrots in his shirt, I had to explain
> he was hungry, somebody took his meat or his porridge away from
> him. So he was punished and, I suppose because I challenged the
> supervisor in front of the whole group, I was punished with him
> . . . . After awhile, I got my rewards for it . . . he'd slip me a carrot
> for a retainer fee. (CHARLIE: 19)

With this behavior, a new role in the sub-culture was defined:
that of the advocate. Even the resistance movement itself had
complexities; along with the advocacy role came a fee for
services.

Eventually, the supervisor decided that this particular person
could be enticed into supporting the system. He was put in
charge of a cleaning team. When his team cleaned so quickly
and efficiently that he could lead them out to the playground
for recreation while the other teams were still working, the
supervisor could not approve.

> It backfired on us. We'd finish in half the time, we'd go off and
> they'd call us back. They added another task to us . . . instead of
> rewarding us . . . . I said [to my gang], 'We were betrayed . . . we'll
> just do ordinary work.' (CHARLIE: 14)

The message to this instigator was clear. Playtime was not an
appropriate occupation for boys who should be cleaning and no
rewards are available for efficient work. One should use all the
time predetermined by staff as necessary to complete the task.
Although he unwillingly co-operated, he saw the system for what
it was: incapable of dealing with efficiency of this nature.

Clique-like gangs were typical of life on the boys' side of the school. The four males interviewed each made reference to the gangs. They defined a life of their own apart from the dictates of the school and over the years operated with only occasional attempts at control by the supervisors. Leo described the groups as follows:

> They weren't that big of a group. The older boys, some of them were dominating the rest of the kids and they had the kids terrorize the younger ones. That was going on all year. They couldn't report it. If they ever reported it to the staff, they would be beat up. They got away with it.

Other comments about the cliques suggested that either the school personnel were unaware of their existence or more likely that they simply ignored what they could not control. By the late fifties, the factions had become more clearly defined and on occasion were extremely competitive.

> See, you had your clans. Every reserve was separate. I had cousins in Bonaparte and Ashcroft so Kamloops and Bonaparte, we really stuck together. Then I was sort of the clique leader. I gradually had Chase brought in and then some of Lytton after that. Just about all of us [intermediate boys] were in: forty-two of us to be exact.
>
> It got pretty hot and heavy—the scrapping. There was one group trying to lead one way and I was leading the other way . . . . The supervisors couldn't do nothing. (SAM: 8)

Eventually the 'scrapping' led to preparations for a major battle for the leadership. When somebody 'squealed', everybody was herded into the recreation room where they were relieved of their weapons including brass knuckles, clubs, and switch-blades. The supervisor's comment was that this was police business, not school business. Eventually the fight did take place under less public circumstances. Sam's final comment on the situation was: "He was doing it just for show . . . . Them forty-two were my people" *(8)*.

Daily, the cliques were involved in less confrontational activities such as sending runners to town to buy alcohol during the Friday night movies and in food theft and other minor 'crimes'. Their success was based on a need by students to feel a sense of belonging and to have some choice about the control of their lives. As the former leader wisely pointed out, "The point [for fighting] only come to the surface once a year. But what it really was, was below the surface in here, [pointing to heart]" *(Sam: 8)*. Strong reaction to the authoritarian environment in which the boys lived exhibited itself at these times, but the boys felt the inhumanity of the system continually.

Charlie, who chose not to become involved in the groups after his initial encounter with "the meanest group of people I ever met in my life," offered this analysis.

> I would imagine that if you're not feeling good about yourself, you begin to look for weaker ones . . . and you get your licks in before time passes by . . . . Those who intended to make fun of us when we started probably were not feeling good about themselves: about their progress, their life. Being sad about leaving the comforts of home just like we were, [they] found us to be the weakest . . . looking back, I thank them for it . . . because it put some strength into us. (6)

He chose to set himself apart and submerse himself in his academic work. Because the nature of the groups changed over the years, generalizations based on any particular time may be somewhat inaccurate. Whether people banded together for mutual support and the sense of family which developed, or if the stronger were establishing and demonstrating their superiority probably varied over time. The gang of intermediate boys described initially fell into the former category in that they originally came together to repel the control of the seniors. As time went on and their strength grew, the excitement of the organization perpetuated it. Within the oppressive system, the gang provided a resistance force, and became oppressors in their own right. People who suffer oppression frequently react by oppressing others. Because the children lived in an inhumane environment, they learned to act in inhumane ways.

Josephine decided that rather than actively resist, in order to survive, she would make herself an integral part of the school system. When she arrived at the residence she quickly realized that co-operation with the nuns would lead her to a place of privilege and some power.

> Once I learned to respect the nuns . . . when you done as you were told and worked hard, you got little promotions. You no longer have to work in the hallways or in the bathrooms. You don't have to scrub anymore. You went up the ladder. You went up in where

the nuns are, their quarters. You started to work there and then from there, you got to graduate to where the priests' quarters are and then into the chapel part where it's cleaner and easier.

Then in the kitchen, too, it's up to you. If you want to remain in the scullery, if you think it's fine, then that's where you stayed, because you're not trying to advance and get into the staff cooking . . . . Cooking for them [the staff] was more fun than cooking for the children . . . . You're accessed to all that beautiful food on the staff side. And if you so like, you can just fill up on there and never mind all that mushed up food. (3-5)

This person attributed her practical approach to life at the school to her parents. Because she was the oldest in a large family, she had always been expected to work very hard—perhaps harder than children with older siblings or those from smaller families. She knew discipline through necessity. Rather than actively resisting the system, she chose to work it to her advantage. In her privileged position, she gained considerable control over her life and as a result developed a sense of self-esteem.

Another form of active resistance was to run away. From the time the school began, children recognized this option. For some it was a thrill and a temporary break from school; for others it was a graphic plea to those at home to save them from their misery. Cecilia, who attended early in the century, recalled:

Gee, one time six girls run away. It was at night; they put the sheets out the window.

They have to [go back]. Somebody look for them on the Indian reserve. They found them down . . . Ben's home. They take them back.

They didn't stay too long: about one day and a half maybe . . . . [They ran away] just for fun, maybe, fed up with going to school. They asked me to go. I told them, 'No, I don't want to go; they'll just bring me back to the school.' I didn't go. (1)

Children who ran away were punished severely: the ones who were brought back had their heads shaved or their hair cut very short. Leo remembered:

They always came back. They got them back. I don't remember anybody getting away completely . . . . Some got expelled; they got

> lashes and then they got expelled . . . . Father had a strap; s about an inch, inch and a half maybe. And there was two bled and they were rivetted together. He used that. (15)

Josephine remembered a specific incident.

> They'd been planning for weeks on end, packing stuff and hiding it outside. And then one night they all went to bed with their nightgown over their clothes . . . . A girlfriend and myself watched all this. How exciting. Anyways they went one by one down the fire escape . . . . There used to be a watchman . . . you could see the light every time he came around the windows . . . so probably these girls timed him . . . . I guess when they got around the corner then they all ran. You could hear them on the rocks . . . . Crazy us, we gave them an hour and then a friend of mine said, 'I'm going to go and knock on sister's door and tell her some of the girls are missing.' It took quite a while; the last one took about a month before they found her. (25)

Although these ones all returned to the school, other runaways, particularly those in later years, did not come back. It was not uncommon for children to run away and be kept home by their parents.

Others were not so lucky. In the school's official registers of 1947, the following note is the final entry for three boys: "Absconded Noon, Sept. 24. Killed in freight wreck Sept. 27" *(Kamloops Indian Residential School, 1947: n.p.).* A student who attended in the early sixties hitchhiked home after running away and was raped. Her parents sent her back to school but, when the resultant pregnancy became evident, she was expelled. Running away was one of the ways students showed their unhappiness. Before the options of day school on reserve or public school, stringent laws forced the return of most of the fugitives.

Parental and political involvement in the school, although infrequently sought or acted upon by the administration, provided support for the children in their resistance to the injustices of the system. In 1913, Chief Louis of Kamloops expressed his dissatisfaction with the school during the proceedings of the now infamous McKenna-McBride commission. As was clearly the case with the move to cut off portions of reserve land, the commissioners, prime examples of Freire's cultural invaders *(1970: 150),* apparently came not to listen but, with their minds already made up, to persuade.

Chief Louis said: . . . I expected to see my people improve when they first went to Industrial School, but I have not seen anything of it. When they come out from school they don't seem to have improved much . . . .

The Chairman: Are you not getting the benefit of that to some extent? For instance can you write?

A. I write in my heart only.

Q. Can you write with a pen?

A. No.

Q. Don't you have to apply now and again to some of these children who have been to school to write for you?

A. Yes.

Q. And that is some help, is it not?

A. Yes.

Q. And some of them can read?

A. Yes, they bring me news.

Q. Well, the school is doing some good then?

A. Well, yes.

The Chairman: I have seen the Indian children go through their examination, and have seen them pass their examinations quite as well as any white children I have ever seen, surely that is improving them, is it not?

A. Yes.

(BRITISH COLUMBIA ROYAL COMMISSION ON INDIAN AFFAIRS, 1913: 15-76)

With that, the recorded interview ended. Rather than seeking to understand Chief Louis's concerns, the chairman showed him that, from the white perspective, improvement was taking place. Needless to say, there was no follow-up to the concerns expressed.

Leo recalled a number of the chiefs visiting the school in the thirties.

There wasn't very many that complained . . . because we knew it wouldn't go out anyway. It was censored. But the odd note got out and so they invited all the chiefs. I know about three times, four times while I was there . . . . Around 1937, '38, they invited all the chiefs from all surrounding areas that had children there . . . . Then they'd give us a decent meal while the chiefs were there. That's no good. (12)

On these visits usually held in response to chiefs' concerns about their children's complaints of hunger, the school personnel made efforts to present themselves in a good light. While it is normal to have good food when guests are invited, the action served to throw doubt on the children's accusations and to calm the parents' apprehensions. In 1946, after much lobbying, Chief Andrew Paull, President of the North American Indian Brotherhood, was permitted to address a parliamentary committee appointed to consider revisions to the Indian Act (*Special Joint Committee, 1946: 419*). He presented Native people's apprehensions about a number of issues including the residential school. Martha recalled:

> Parents were beginning to complain about the way the children were being fed and . . . the way their children were being treated . . . . The Indian people themselves started fighting for integration. Then in 1945, we got together with the late Andy Paull . . . and from then on we started fighting against residential schools . . . . They fought for better education; they fought for better treatment. They found out a lot of these young people . . . didn't have no chance in life unless they were [from] a strong family or you were a strong person . . . . You had to be told what time to eat, what time to go to bed, what time to bath, what time to change, all this type of thing. (22-24)

Through political action, stimulated by their own and their children's experiences at the school, the twenty year campaign to close the school began.

On another occasion, strong action on the part of the parents had immediate effect. The children were upset by the cruel treatment they were receiving at the hands of the music instructor.

> We had been sneaking letters home to our parents [about] how we were being treated here . . . . The Chief from home came one weekend with two other chiefs. They came and . . . we went to the parlour and visited with him. He told us what they were planning to do, said, 'If anybody gets beat up again by this Mr. _____, we want to know about it.'
>
> So this one night we were all down in the dining room and we were practicing hymns. And girls were getting irritated because he said he wasn't satisfied . . . . And this was getting towards midnight and we were getting tired. He went along to the senior bench and

he listened. He put his ear right down to their mouth and A_____ wasn't even singing. She was mad. There was another girl . . . . He slapped A_____ but [the other girl] . . . answered him back and that just blew him. He hit her with the harmonica and she started bleeding. It split her head. And that's when everybody started screaming and they all ran out when they seen blood. And he just went wild, grabbed her and shook the hell out of her.

And she ran . . . . Within two days, [the chiefs] were here . . . . And I remember . . . [one] attacking the guy. He told him if he didn't leave the school that he would charge him . . . . And I remember that old guy leaving.

The next year he came back in a brother suit: he became a brother . . . . And . . . [the chief] came again when we told him that this Mr. _____ is a brother . . . and he is back. And the chief came and really raised hell with him, told him 'I don't care if you come camouflaged in a priest suit . . . we told you to leave. We don't want you back. Get!' He disappeared and we've never seen him since. (SOPHIE: 3)

Although local politicians and parents had little power to affect the everyday life of the school, in extreme incidents such as the one described, they took power and wielded it forcefully. This moral support helped the children deal with the hardships of everyday life and inspired them to continue to believe in their people's strength.

Parents also became directly involved in their children's welfare. One person described her parents' horror at the head shaving and kerosene treatment her sister had received. The kerosene had burned the girl's head. As the children and parents were commiserating in the parlour during a family visit, the hapless priest walked in: "Dad just grabbed him and shook him up" (Linda: 2). The irate father tried to relieve his sense of helpless frustration caused by his daughter's plight. Linda described another visit by her parents. She was on a special diet to prevent allergies.

They tried to make me eat what everybody else was eating . . . . I wouldn't eat so she made that plate sit there until the next meal and I still wouldn't eat . . . . This went on for four meals . . . . We snuck a letter out . . . . So the next day, my mum and dad both came . . . . They knew we were eating so they just walked right down to that room . . . . My dad walked into where the nuns and priests were eating . . . and he said to that priest, 'And you expect my daughter to eat this slop and you guys are in there eating like kings and queens.' (31)

Following the ensuing altercation, all agreed that the special diet would be re-instated. Again the child was given a sense of having some rights in an apparently inhumane environment.

The pockets of resistance were significant at the Kamloops Indian Residential School. Those students not directly involved in opposing the rules and regulations were few. At times, the oppression produced counter-cultures: groups of children who defined roles, projects, and ways of daily life for and with one another. They did so without the sanction, and in some cases, without even the knowledge of those who officially held the power of administration. Although other aspects of the school also influenced the children's development, these opposition movements live clearly in people's memories as times of strength. Fascination and fear are recurring themes for people discussing the sub-cultures. There is wonder at the inventiveness of the children, and the complexities of the roles which developed, there is fear for the recklessness of those involved and the extents to which students went to define their versions of power and control. At the same time, not one interviewee involved in the thievery, the gang warfare, or the other forms of resistance indicated any sense of regret for their actions. In retrospect, these actions can be viewed as the actions of strong people against a system which degraded and dehumanized.

CHAPTER 5

GOING HOME

"Who are you, who are you? I have to admit to them, to myself I am an Indian."

Frances Katasse (1969: xi)

Eventually the time came for leaving school. Some students were sent home when they became ill. Others who ran away were allowed to stay home. Some students, those who died at the school, never went home.

> She was a really good friend. Tattooing your hands [was common]. And she done that, she used a common pin or needle . . . and wrote her initials on her hand and then it got blood poisoning from the ink. Like her hand was swelling and swelling. Two or three days later . . . she started getting a fever.
>
> So she showed the nun and they just sent her to bed. And when she must have been in bed about two days . . . she was getting so she wasn't even herself. . . . And she just lay in bed and two days later she died. (LINDA: 26)

Other reports of death by those interviewed include one accidental death by hanging when some children left a playmate who was pretending to be an outlaw. The box he was standing on slipped from under him when no one was there. By the time someone noticed him missing from school, it was too late. Children who became ill with scarlet fever, tuberculosis, and other diseases were sent home or to hospitals. Many never returned to school.

Others left school when they reached the final grade offered: for many years, it was grade eight. From 1951-1959, when high school was included, some people graduated. Beginning in 1960, high school students attended school at St. Ann's Academy in Kamloops *(Kamloops Souvenir Edition, 1977: 4, 10)*.

Most students interviewed credit the school with making them tough. In answer to the question "What did you learn in school?," Sam replied, "To watch yourself and independence"

(3). Needless to say, the academic subjects were of lesser importance to him. Sophie summed up her experience in this way:

> All in all my life hasn't really been that bad. It is just knowing I
> went through that humiliation and that hurt, that low self-esteem
> and having come out of it. And never letting that hate leave a scar
> on me. I don't hate anymore . . . . I do get angry but it doesn't
> mean I hate anybody . . . . That's the strength I got from what I
> went through. In a lot of ways I have this place [K.I.R.S.] and the
> people that put me through it to thank for the strength I got . . .
> a lot of strength to fight back and that strength I got is what's made
> me into the woman I am today. (14)

Charlie concurred:

> In retrospect, there are times when I thank them [the tough boys]
> for it because they put fight into me physically and mentally. They
> helped make me mentally tough because I met other tough situa-
> tions which were not as tough as that . . . . And having survived
> that, I think I can survive anything. (6)

For other students the school's stern discipline was at least
temporarily effective. As Nancy said, "My experience in residential school made me a passive, obedient person" *(11)*. She felt
strongly the oppressive nature of the onslaught against her
culture.

> I would sum it up by saying that they were definitely stripping us
> of our culture . . . . There might have been workers who didn't
> know exactly what was happening but they had to follow rules.
> There was no doubt that they were driving out the culture. (4-5)

Some of the lessons had effects opposite to those intended.

> They stress religion over everything else . . . . Going to church was
> more important to them than the classes . . . . The religion part
> was habit . . . . It was just a thing you done day in and day out. If
> those kids would suddenly have to go and pray on the side of a
> mountain by themselves, they wouldn't know how . . . . I think
> when they were saying their grace for their meal, they were looking
> at what kind of ugly stuff they were getting . . . . Mass was cele-
> brated in Latin and we didn't know what we were saying . . . . It's
> just like a punishment going to church. (LEO: 18-19)

This man commented also that he'd learned more about life

while in the army than he did in school. "In the school, we didn't learn anything about life, other than read, and write, and arithmetic, and a low grade, and going to church" *(Leo: 18)*.

When people were finished school and returned home, some re-adjusted quickly to their family's ways. Sophie, always a keen learner, found going home exciting.

> I went home and I stayed home with my mother. I helped . . . gathering foods and learning how to dry salmon . . . experiencing the type of food and the [time of] year that they ate. I had to acquire the taste to it because I had forgotten it after so many years . . . . I found that I'm easy to adjust to things and I'm always aware this was an experience I wanted to learn. I wanted to know how did my parents survive here in the winter. (11)

For a few, the idea of succeeding in the larger society was combined with the idea of being Shuswap. Charlie, who was hesitating about his plans for life after graduation, received strong words of advice from an elder.

> I complained, 'I would like to be a doctor or a teacher but I'm just an Indian and Indians don't become doctors.' And I'd keep on this. 'I would like to go to big school, university they call it . . . There's nobody there who's Indian.'
>
> She was a little tiny woman. She jumped up and stamped her feet . . . . She said, 'That's an excuse . . . . You have hands, you have a mind, you have people who lived long before you who had a control of life . . . . That is Indian. That is Shuswap. You have it flowing through your veins . . . . It is because you are an Indian that you do well whatever you do . . . .' (12)

This advice was instrumental in giving Charlie the strength to accept his Indianness with pride, and to build a successful and happy life on that foundation.

For others, cultural clashes surfaced. For the women who left in the forties, arranged marriages were the focus of conflict. Josephine, who returned to work at the school to avoid her parents' decision, enlisted her brother's support. He said:

> 'Write to Father _____. We'll write him a letter and we'll tell him all about it. You don't want to get married and you want to keep on going to school . . . . ' So both of us . . . wrote a long letter . . . and quite a few days later, my mum and dad got a letter that I was to return to school. And my mum was very angry. (9)

Sophie eventually married the person her mother had chosen. However, she did so when she felt ready and only after spending considerable time working.

> Still I was yearning for more learning. After one year at home . . . . I guess the reason I wanted to get out of there was my mother wouldn't leave me rest: I had to get married. But I didn't want to; I wasn't ready yet . . . . I wanted to know what it was to be independent. And I fought my mother; I rebelled against her. (4, 12)

Sophie worked for different families in the area as a housekeeper and began learning in earnest.

> The one thing I stole from the school . . . was an old torn up dictionary . . . .
>
> The thing that I learned when I was with them [the people I worked for], we used to sit around the breakfast table and dinner table and I used to pay attention to their conversation. I'd hear a word. One word that always sticks in my mind. . .was the word naive. I thought, 'Gee, that's a new word.' After I finished eating, I excused myself, I ran up to my bedroom. I looked through my dictionary and I studied how you spell it and how you pronounce it and what is the meaning. Then a few days later, I'd try to use it in my own conversation . . . .
>
> And there were many words after that . . . . I read books one after another . . . and I began to learn. I learned how to express myself and I learned how to talk a little better than I learned in here [K.I.R.S.]. (4)

Although the reading skills she had learned in school allowed her to proceed in this way, unfortunately school had never provided an opportunity for this kind of investigative and stimulating education. For her, significant learning began only after she left the oppressive system and found a new sense of purpose and self-worth.

For both Josephine and Sophie, defying their parents' wishes for immediate marriage was in all likelihood based on their experiences at school. Whether it was a part of the school's tactics to attack the idea of arranged marriages, or if it had merely taught them defiance, is an interesting question. Nevertheless, both women did defy their parents' wishes. Neither mentioned any influence from the school regarding arranged marriages. However, because Europeans had discontinued the practice, one may assume that the school personnel would oppose the idea and consequently support the women in their opposition to the tradition.

The whole area of sexuality provided another focus for clashes. The children had been taught in school to de-emphasize sexuality. In traditional Shuswap life, it was viewed as a natural part of life. Martha, who attended school for only three years, described her grandmother's teachings about sex.

> When I was growing up and getting into womanhood, [Granny] told me . . . . 'You got a beautiful body; you look after that body . . . . Don't abuse it.' She told me about the facts of life; she told me how to cleanse my body . . . . I'd look at myself and I'd say to myself ' . . . Granny always says my body is beautiful. Look after it with great respect.' (17)

In direct contrast to this acceptance of the physical self, the religious people at school insisted in covering the body at all times. Women reported that they were told to wear their underwear in the shower, and that their breasts were never to be seen, even as they changed clothes. Sex was not a topic of discussion in the school.

> The nuns were really pathetic . . . . Later on as an adult, I talked to them. They said, 'We thought you kids knew lots,' because we came from the reserve. And we knew nothing. (MARY: 16)

Anne, who attended school ten years later, found what she learned about sex had tremendous repercussions in her life.

> I was really scared . . . . Every time I went to the washroom . . . it's wrong. You better not touch yourself . . . . If I looked at somebody: . . . lust, sex, and I got scared of those sexual feelings. And I didn't know how to handle them . . . .
>
> What really confused me was if intercourse was a sin, why are people born? . . . . It took me a really long time to get over the fact that . . . . I've sinned: I had a child. (13)

Although both traditional Shuswap and Catholic religions emphasized that sex should be confined to marriage, the methods for presenting these views are contradictory. Traditional Shuswap values emphasize the positive: that the body is beautiful and should be cared for accordingly.

> I've always been a Shuswap and I've always been a woman. I looked
> after myself and I always believe that where my children come
> from, that's like a temple. (MARY: 16)

The Catholic controls described by informants stressed the
negative: sex is closely tied with sin; daily contact with the
opposite sex can lead to sin in thought, word, or deed. Consis-
tent with the tyrannical controls imposed by the school personnel, the threats of sin and hell fire were visualized as appropriate
means of minimizing sexual thoughts of any kind. Other than
these threats, the most common control was to ignore the
existence of sexuality—to cover bodies and never to mention the
topic. This negativism clashed with Shuswap ideas and for a
number of the people interviewed created problems which
required careful resolution in later life.

Native languages were another significant issue for people
going home. As has been noted, the use of Shuswap, Thompson,
Chilcotin, or any other Native language was forbidden in the
school. Although second generations attending the residential
school frequently did not speak their language, the first generation managed to maintain their knowledge at least partially.
Many who started school at nine or ten have either retained
their fluency, or regained it with the recent developing awareness of the significance of language to culture. Those who left
school in the earlier years found some need to readjust to using
the language. Leo commented:

> You know something funny about speaking your own language.
> When I first come out of school, I was embarrassed to speak my
> language in front of white people . . . . Now I speak Shuswap any
> place and any time . . . but it took about three or four years . . . to
> get away from that embarrassment of speaking it on the street
> . . . . They just about brainwashed us out of it. (22)

Within these words lie a clear indication of the intent by the
school to eradicate the Native people's language. Not only were
students forbidden to speak it in school, they were also convinced that their use of the language was an indication of
inferiority. The import attached to public humiliation for
Shuswap people has already been discussed. In this case, it was
included in the indoctrination which was hoped would serve as
a control even after people had left the direct influence of its
perpetrators.

The fact that some people did not manage to resist these controls is indisputable. Although one person who continues to speak his language puzzled about those who swore that they had forgotten how to speak their language, Linda shed some interesting light on the subject.

> I spoke Indian when I went to school. I could speak some English because [my sisters] went to school. So you learnt. They told you when they came back . . . . 'You can't speak Indian; you got to speak English. If you speak Indian, you get whipped.' It took them a long time to get it out of me. And to this day . . . . I speak some words . . . but I don't speak it fluently. I used to be able to speak it fluently before I went to school. (36)

She then described her recent attendance at a spiritual sweat ceremony in which she could temporarily speak her language fluently. The possibility exists that psychological controls developed by the school prevent her from speaking it. If this is the case, then the possibility also exists that some key, perhaps therapy to create understanding of the system which 'got it out of her,' might enable her to speak the language again. Discussion with Charlie who has returned to his language after time away confirms this possibility.

> Most of my Shuswap was learned from birth to the time I come to school . . . . And I left the language until ten years ago. That's roughly a period of thirty years when I didn't have the language spoken. I spoke intermittently with some elders but when I returned to the language I had no difficulty at all. I'm fluent. I was fluent when I was eight and I teach the language now. (5)

Mary, who commented "I shouldn't even say I'm proud; I had to put words to it. It's my language; it's who I am," provided more insight into the notion that a language learned in childhood remains buried in the mind.

> There are a lot of words I haven't said yet, but it's in my computer [brain]. I found that out last year: I never said 'Sl' gh gee' and yet I know it. I never said it through my mouth . . . . There's a lot of words in there I haven't said through my mouth yet because those were put in when I didn't need to use those words. Now as an adult I need to use them. (14)

For those who came to school with their language, their chances

of retention were relatively good, particularly with summer
visits to reinforce its use. Perhaps the school's biggest effect on
language use could be called secondary: although punishing
children for speaking their language did not eradicate it, as
adults many consciously did not teach their children a Native
language so that they might avoid the punishments incurred
through its use at school. Others believed the propaganda
designed to convince them that Shuswap was unimportant. This
generational control has had devastating effects on the children
whose parents attended residential school. Many of them have
never learned their Native language.

For many people who attended K.I.R.S. the religious teachings
lead to confusion and lack of faith.

> There was a lot of times I used to wonder why God didn't answer
> my prayers. People said if you pray, God will hear you. It seemed
> like I prayed so much, I used to pray to go home and . . . you just
> couldn't go home. I used to wonder what kind of God it was . . . .
> It was hard to take religion. (ALICE: 7)

Alice has since moved away from the Catholic Church which
had little meaning for her. Others have managed to combine
their Catholic beliefs with traditional ones.

> I'm a Catholic today, a practicing Catholic. And whatever I believe
> from my ancestry is real and I believe in that. I want to live as best
> I could . . . . On my own spiritualism of my people, I know there
> was something there and I know it's real . . . .
>
> They [Catholic and traditional religions] are not [mutually
> exclusive] especially if you get away from the mortal sin and God's
> going to punish you . . . . God is love. He made each of us. (MARY:
> 16)

This positive approach to adaptation of the two ways of spirituality has led this person to a peaceful resolution of conflicts
between the two.

Not all people who attended the Kamloops Indian Residential School managed to reach such a compromise. Former
students who are now parents recognize the deficiencies in their
experience with family units. Alice commented, "The residential schools took away the responsibility of the parents because
the parents didn't see the kids all year" (1). Children learn
parenting skills by the way they are parented. Those who spent

eight, ten or more years at K.I.R.S. had limited experience as family members. In the same way that their language use is based on the knowledge they gained before going to school, so their parenting skills must draw on that limited experience.

Alcohol also became a force in the lives of some families. Some parents, heartbroken at the loss of their children and objects of continuing oppression from all aspects of the dominant society escaped these pressures with alcohol. For some children alcohol became the norm on visits home.

> When we started coming home at Christmas time . . . it was one big party. Even us kids got involved with the drinking. We sat there and got as drunk as everybody else did . . . . When I think about it, we really . . . blame[d] Mum a lot for what happened. And I think that's probably another reason why she started drinking was she thought we didn't need her anymore. (LINDA: 23)

This person saw two forces related to school as contributing to her mother's alcoholism. Her mother felt unneeded, and in all likelihood felt that the children blamed her for sending them to school. She would have, on the one hand, the children pleading to stay home, and on the other hand, the government and church insisting that she send them to school. A desire to escape from these inescapable pressures is understandable.

Suicide, the ultimate escape from a harsh reality, was another route taken by despairing people. Although none of the people interviewed mentioned victims of suicide, Alice contemplated it when her life appeared to be without meaning.

> I started to think, 'Well, twelve years here. I don't want to be here for twelve years.' By the time I was in grade five, they used to let us go for walks . . . . I decided . . . to go down to the Thompson River . . . [It] was really high; it was spring time, I guess and you could see that the water was deep and I don't know how many times . . . I used to think of drowning myself. I would be standing there and I would think 'Gee, life can't continue like this.' (5)

While blame for Native suicides cannot be laid entirely with the residential school, it can be seen as a contributing factor to people's confusion over values and the meaning of life, and symptomatic of the social oppression which may lead to such attempts.

Perhaps one of the reasons for the strength of the people

interviewed for this study lies with the fact that the words and ways of the elders and of their families still have tremendous influence on their lives and the lives of many Shuswap people. Despite the years of residential schooling, parental and cultural values remained strong within the students' psyches.

> [Granny] had dreams. Before, I guess through my Catholic teaching, I thought dreams and all these other things were wrong like sin. But in praying about it in my adult life . . . we all have those powers. I've come to believe that. (MARY: 11)

Traditional ways are integral parts of the lives of most of the people interviewed. Mary also commented:

> All the people from our way teach us never use food in an argument . . . . You don't withhold food or abuse it in an argument. Food is sustenance. (12)

Anne feels her grandmother's presence in the house which she inherited from her.

> Her spirit is really strong in the house. Sometimes if I neglect to do something, she lets me know, or sometimes if I get balky . . . she's got enough patience, she'll wait until I'm ready because I sometimes get scared of what she is trying to teach me. (11)

Anne described burning sage in her house as a cleansing technique which she had learned by watching her grandmother. "I just watched her. She never told me nothing. She'd just get it and burn it" *(10)*. Mary describes a custom her grandmother used with her that she now uses with her own grandchildren.

> I remember her doing that to me [gesturing] and saying, 'Whsst, whsst.' That was like every evening. And other times she would pat my hair . . . . I think she talked to me those times but she used to always do that, 'Whsst, whsst.' I always find that funny. I do that to my grandchildren. I wonder what that was all about, but my kya a used to do that to me. (10)

Although apparently insignificant little details in life, it is this unquestioning acceptance that this is the way people do things which forms some of the basis for cultural identity and strength. As another grandmother was being interviewed, her grandchildren, young adults, sat at a nearby kitchen table preparing pine needles for 'Granny's medicine.' In many ways, the traditions are perpetuated.

In the final analysis, the people interviewed for this study are survivors. The alcoholism and the suicide statistics speak to the suffering and pain of many who attended the school and conversely to the strength of those survivors. The study participants who were subjected to a massive onslaught against their culture and all it stood for have—in a demonstration of the strength of the human spirit—grown, changed, developed and at the same time remained conscious of their ancestry.

Throughout the years, the survivors have resisted the cultural invasion around them. The people who attended K.I.R.S. were indubitably changed by their experience. However, neither government policy nor missionary fervour to assimilate the Indians was successful. Through pain, hunger, cold, and corporal punishment, the people interviewed managed to remain their ancestors' children and to glean understanding of the importance of being Native as an irrepressible part of life.

CHAPTER 6
EPILOGUE

"The government asks Indians, 'What do you want?'
But they don't understand we're different cultures and
have different answers to the question."
> Marina Tom
> *Wisdom of the Elders*
> *(Kirk, 1986)*

The most outstanding notion which emerges from these stories of Native people attending the Kamloops Indian Residential School is the extent and complexity of their resistance. The students in their wisdom recognized the injustice of the system which attempted to control them and to transform them. In innumerable ways, they fought for some control in an impersonalized system: for decent daily lives without cold and hunger, and for the means to survive the oppression around them while maintaining a sense of self and family. This strength has led to today's work in education by Native people throughout British Columbia.

The struggles at the Kamloops Indian Residential School were struggles for power and control, as the invaders and the resistance clashed with one another over these issues. European teachers and priests, strong in their belief in hierarchy and the superiority of their cultures, attempted to annihilate Native cultures and to absorb the children of those cultures into their power structure. Inherent in the notion of hierarchy within capitalism is the possibility of rising to a position of superiority. Rarely acknowledged by the proponents of the system is that this myth allows for a few in the upper echelons while the masses struggle amongst themselves against the hegemony which the system perpetrates. For one to win, the others must lose. In the residential school, the message given to the students was clearly that they, because of their history, were inferior.

Cultural invasion as discussed and revealed in the stories presented here is one means of imposing a power structure: in this case, the Europeans attempted to impose their hierarchical model upon members of another distinct cultural group, the Native people of the Kamloops area. The policy makers and implementors of both the government and the church adhered to the notion of their superiority in dealing with Native children. They knew what was best in almost all regards. Their experiences with life were significant and to be acted upon; the students' experiences were devalued and dismissed.

Both Church and government are themselves oligarchies. Within the Catholic church, the Pope is the ultimate authority and other officials fall clearly into position beneath him. Obedience to superiors is an essential aspect of the church's established order. Though less dogmatic, government is structured similarly. Within departments the ministers hold the ultimate influence. Too often, they depend on the views of people within their immediate environs for information on which they establish policy direction. Occasionally in an effort to simulate input from the people at the community level, predetermined alternatives are presented for consideration and decision-making—a mockery of free choice. Actions such as these, reminiscent of the days of benevolent despots, typify the Department of Indian Affairs' ideas on Native input in education and other areas to the present day. Some bands, in efforts to combat the continuing lack of sensitivity to their needs, are taking more control of their children's education through strong political action and community involvement. The resistance which was exemplified at residential school continues to grow.

In 1987, the buildings which housed the Kamloops Indian Residential School for so many years stand as an historical reminder of the nature of Native education since the Europeans first arrived. However, unlike many others which have been abandoned, fallen into disrepair or even burned, these buildings are a hive of activity, a tribute to the survival of the Secwepemc people, a microcosm of the world of Native control and Native education today. A tour of the buildings reveals a fascinating collection of political and educational enterprises.

The senior girls' dormitory on the top floor of the east wing is now a field centre for the Native Indian Teacher Education Program (N.I.T.E.P.), a University of B.C. program for prospective elementary teachers. Directly below is the college preparation program, organized by the Secwepemc Cultural Education

Society, and now threatened by funding cutbacks by the Department of Indian Affairs. A Native Adult Basic Education Program is offered. On the main floor, a band operated child care centre, Little Fawn Day Care, is thriving. It caters to Native people who work and study in the various offices of the building, and to people from Kamloops who drive their children across the river. A qualified band member runs the centre; several other Kamloops band members are employed. After-school care is available for children attending the band-run school next door. In the basement, a Montessori school, run and predominately attended by non-Natives, rents facilities from the band.

To the west is an efficient cafeteria. The women who come to cook and organize the facilities attended the residential school as students. Much of the kitchen equipment from their school days is still in use. Now it is used to prepare meals for elders' gatherings; for a variety of conferences such as the one held in 1986 to discuss British Columbia's Master Tuition Agreement, a contentious bilateral agreement between federal and provincial governments; and for thrice-weekly meals for students and workers in the complex. The meals served in the infamous dining room include bannock on a regular basis, salmon, and at least once, a sampling of steamed lichen. Across from the large dining room, which also serves as a meeting hall for graduation celebrations and school Christmas concerts, is the smaller "priests' dining room." It has a continuous supply of coffee for the maintenance staff and is used for lunches when fewer people are about during school holidays.

Up the centre stairs from the cafeteria are a variety of offices used by groups like the now disbanded Central Interior Tribal Council (C.I.T.C.). This group separated over time, as local control became an issue of increasing importance and the centralized nature of the group was felt to be inefficient. The now-deserted chapel is also located on this floor. Although it is still used occasionally for weddings and funerals, most of the Catholic ceremonies have moved to the recently restored heritage church in what was the central village of the reserve. A salmon enhancement project; the Western Indian Agriculture Corporation; and an underfunded but well-stocked resources centre, a vestige of the C.I.T.C., occupy the remainder of the floor. At the top of the central stairs is the Shuswap Nation

Tribal Council, a very active political organization of the Shuswap bands of the area.

At the west end of the building, one can climb a flight of stairs to the Secwepemc Cultural Education Society. This extremely active group has many responsibilities. The director of the museum and archives has initiated the return of artifacts from other museums. Primary research for educational and political purposes is conducted by workers in the centre. A curriculum committee is finalizing two supplementary texts, which focus on Secwepemc experiences, for elementary schools. A desktop publishing company is being developed. A media centre has produced a number of videos in conjunction with the Society's activities. A series of workshops focusing on a variety of skills, from researching techniques to writing and publishing, have been held. Shuswap language teachers have participated in a number of professional development days organized here. Above the cultural centre, the empty senior boys' dorm awaits a new idea or project.

To the south of the large brick main building is the 'new' dormitory. Most recently, it was rented by the Kamloops Christian School for their classes. An independent school, it did attract a few Native students whose parents have chosen to remove their students from the public schools and who feel that religious training is important. While some classes follow the B.C. curriculum, the older students use the ACE program, an American Christian correspondence program which focuses on Christian values.

To the west of the main building lies the classroom block of the residential school. This building now includes the Little Fawn Nursery School and the three classrooms of the Sek'lep Elementary School. The former is completely band administered and staffed. The latter, a responsibility of the local school district, was initiated by the band and has major band input in both hiring and staffing. All of the buildings were turned over to the band in 1977; since then they have been of increasing importance both culturally and economically. Plans for major re-organization and development of the buildings have been completed. Ironically, those buildings which for so long were the centre of a cultural onslaught are now the centre of cultural enhancement and economic development.

Although residential schools served as one of the strongest

tools used by Euro-Canadians in their efforts to assimilate Native people, their closure clearly did not signal an end to the ongoing struggle for cultural recognition and meaningful education by the diverse Native groups in British Columbia. Even as the residential schools operated, some Native groups had successfully insisted on the establishment of day schools on reserve. These were operated by the Department of Indian Affairs. Officials and teachers complained that children's attendance was erratic, and parents worried about the quality of the teachers and the curriculum. But the day schools, some of which continue to this day on a few reserves, met the federal requirements of compulsory attendance and provided an alternative to residential school. Other parents chose to enfranchise. They gave up their rights as aboriginal people and moved off-reserve so that their children could attend public schools. Some people felt that the provincial schools were superior to both residential and federal day schools.

After much lobbying by Native people, major revisions to the Indian Act in 1951 included the option for Native children to attend public schools. Funding agreements between individual school districts and the federal government made throughout the decade were eventually formalized and generalized as the Master Tuition Agreement in British Columbia. Negotiated solely between the federal and provincial governments, it has been a bone of contention among Native people for many years. It did, however, allow for the attendance of Native children in the public school system which was expected to serve as the answer to Native children's educational needs. The assumption that treating Native children the same as non-Native children would provide them with an equal education went unquestioned at this time. While there was little overt prediction of the effects of integration, it appears that people assumed that teaching the same content in the same ways to Native and non-Native students would provide their children with the same opportunities for employment and further education. No acknowledgement was given to differing life experiences and cultural backgrounds. These are now seen as significant in determining students' needs and the direction which schooling should take as a result. Failure by everyone concerned to recognize the extent to which ethnocentrism and racism permeate Canadian society further complicated matters.

For some Native children, public schooling did serve as a key to progress. But for the vast majority, the culture shock first perpetrated in residential school continued in other forms in the public schools. Students frequently found themselves in classrooms with white middle-class teachers who had little or no understanding of or experience with cross-cultural differences, or the skills to cross the cultural boundaries between them and the Native students. Curricula which focussed on Euro-Canadian issues and which belittled or more frequently ignored Native roles in Canadian society did little to enhance Native students' self-esteem and desire for knowledge. A substitute teacher tells of a Native student working on a history project in the hallway of a public elementary school. She was to research nineteenth century modes of transportation, using The World Book accounts of steam engines. When he questioned her about her grandparents, she demonstrated her knowledge of nineteenth century Native modes of transportation on the Northwest coast. But this was not part of the recognized curriculum and consequently was not given attention in the classroom. In the words of Alvin and Bert McKay of the Nisga'a School District, "No attempt was ever made to involve the people of the Nass in the content of the school courses. Instead, teachers, curriculum guides, texts, and materials were brought in . . . . " (McKay and McKay, 1987: 71). Most importantly, cultural behaviour patterns of teachers and students frequently differed radically and limited communication. The National Indian Brotherhood summed up its concerns in this way:

> . . . it has been the Indian student who was asked to integrate: to give up his identity, to adopt new values and a new way of life . . . . (1973: 25-26)

Even on the playground, Native children faced hostility and outright racism.

The National Indian Brotherhood's policy statement, *Indian Control of Indian Education* (1972), served as a major turning point in Native education in Canada. Issued partly as a response to an unacceptable white paper circulated by the Department of Indian Affairs, it emphasized the significance of local control and parental involvement in Native children's education. One of the authors stated in a later paper:

> Our aim is to affect a true sense of identity for ourselves by recognizing traditional values while simultaneously preparing ourselves to function effectively in the larger society. (KIRKNESS, 1978: 80)

Although some culturally-relevant classrooms and programs existed prior to the Brotherhood's policy paper, it served to focus the attention of both governments and Native people themselves on some issues of fundamental importance to Native students.

Following closely the Indian control statement, in the late seventies, statistics showing Native students' lack of success in public schools began to surface with regularity. The 94% drop-out rate for Native students between kindergarten and grade twelve *(Hawthorn, 1967: 130)* was consistently quoted. At the same time, people recognized that lack of positive role models was proving detrimental to Native students. Consequently, within the province, Native groups, such as the B.C. Native Indian Teachers' Association and established educational institutions, worked to develop programs designed to encourage Native people to consider teaching as a career. One such program is the Native Indian Teacher Education Program, started in 1974 at the University of British Columbia. The proposal for the program pointed out that there were, at that time, twenty-four Native teachers in the province. If teachers were represented in proportion to the general population, there should have been 1,300.

Throughout the seventies, Native parents began to have a greater impact on their children's education. Indian education committees made up of concerned parents and politicians formed on reserves and in school districts. Home-school co-ordinators served as official links between the community and the school. In Williams Lake, Phyllis Chelsea ran for school board and was elected. In northern B.C. in 1974, the Nisga'a established the first Native school district in the province. Native language programs, often taught by community members, began on reserves and in public schools. One parent who expressed interest in a language program for a federal school was recruited by the regular teacher and began the following Monday what became a seven year teaching stint. Funded by the Special Education Branch of B.C.'s provincial education department, co-ordinators of Native education, Native students' counsellors, and Native teacher aides began work in schools and districts with significant Native populations.

Most of the foregoing reforms were implemented within the pre-existing educational systems—either the federally-operated D.I.A. schools, or within the provincially funded and administered public schools. In the eighties, a new form of school emerged. The subject of long discussion, band-run schools were a significant change from the earlier forms of schooling available to Native students. Although they depended for the most part on federal funds, the actual administration of the schools, including hiring practices and curricular choices, was the reponsibility of the band concerned. Opting to move outside existing systems in order to make real changes to the control of their children's schooling, the members of these bands took on a major task. Mt. Currie, Alkali Lake, Canim Lake and Bella Coola are just a few of the bands in B.C. which followed this route.

In Kamloops in 1981, the band decided to make a different kind of change and to move into control in a more gradual way. In co-operation with the local school district, the band opened Sek'lep School. Hiring Shuswap teachers has been a priority and in most years, at least two of the three teachers have been Shuswap. In addition, a Shuswap language teacher and teacher aide have worked in the school. The teachers focus on the provincial curriculum but emphasize Shuswap content wherever possible. The school has grown from its initial single classroom and three grades to three classrooms with all elementary grades.

Parents of five to seven year olds who were interviewed in 1983 generally felt very positive about the school, primarily because their children were happy there. Many of the children had attended day care or nursery school in the same building and, because it is next door to the band office, all are familiar with their surroundings. Comments such as, "He really likes school now," and "She never wants to miss a day," were most common. One parent who had sent her child to the school on a trial basis for kindergarten is very happy with her child's progress, particularly with the Shuswap language program. Another parent had watched her child change from a stubborn and unco-operative child in public kindergarten to a happy grade one student at Sek'lep. In Kamloops, he had been teased about

the length of his hair and had learned that some consider being
Indian as negative. In the band school, he was taught to be
proud of his heritage. His mother commented of the
Secwepemc classroom teacher, "She knows what it's like to be
Indian." The conflict of values which she felt strongly when her
son was in kindergarten had ceased to exist. Children's awareness of issues of political importance to Native people are
discussed in the school. One child reported that when the
students on occasion exchanged insults with the non-Native
children at the nearby religious school, the Native children
reminded the others that they were on Indian land.

The number of band-operated schools is increasing. In 1983,
there were 183 band schools in Canada, compared to 170
federal schools. Sixteen percent of the Native students in Canada were attending band-run schools *(Canadian Education Association, 1984: 13-14)*. In 1984, there were 187 schools enrolling
twenty-three percent of Native students *(Barman et al, 1986: 7)*.
In B.C., hiring flexibility remains one of the attractions. Although Native teachers with full provincial qualifications were
hired as classroom teachers, one band hired a community
member as principal. His history with and understanding of the
community was deemed more important than a university degree for keeping the school meaningful for both children and
their parents.

Because of Native adolescents' lack of success with the
schools generally, adult education programs are of particular
importance. Many who left school without graduating choose
to return to formal education as adults. While adult education
programs have been in operation for decades, since the seventies there have been clear moves by Native people to increase
their influence in this sphere as well. The programs specifically
for Native adults vary from upgrading to vocational training and
university courses such as teacher education and law. Recent
developments include a focus on science and health careers.

Like the schooling for children, the institutions and organi-
zations which offer programs for adults follow one of two
routes. Some reformers choose to operate within exisiting institutions. Others, in search of more radical change, choose to
establish programs outside the control of the dominant society.
There are, of course, advantages and disadvantages to both.
Reform may have significance for the entire existing institution.

As adaptations are made to include Native students, the institution itself is changed. On the other hand, working in an independent institution allows for greater variation in processes and more flexibility in addressing needs specific to the students. A major disadvantage of some independent institutions is that although the education offered may be sound and effective, established institutions refuse to recognize courses or give credit for them to students who want to continue their studies in those institutions.

Within B.C.'s provincially recognized institutions, the college preparation course offered by Fraser Valley College in Chilliwack is a program which appeals to Native students and makes specific attempts to address students' needs while preparing them for success in future college work. N.I.T.E.P. and the Native Law program, both offered by the University of B.C., work to combine the best of both worlds—support systems as needed, with all the regular requirements of a degree program. The Native Education Centre in Vancouver, which has only recently affiliated with Vancouver Community College, operates relatively independently. Run by a non-profit society consisting of a Native board and staffed predominantly by Native people, the Centre offers programs from Native business management to upgrading, computer programming, and college preparation. While building on the strengths of the Native students who come there, the staff also recognizes that students may want to continue their education at other non-Native institutions and structure their courses of study accordingly.

In the Kamloops area, a number of Native controlled educational institutions offer programs to Native adults. In 1986-87, the Secwepemc Cultural Education Society offered an upgrading program purchased from the Native Education Centre, and a college preparation program. The Native Training Institute, operating out of nearby Spences Bridge, emphasizes a life skills approach to formal learning. While offering courses labelled English, Sociology, and Psychology, along with content, the instructors emphasize student involvement, Native perspectives, and Native process. Almost all staff are Native. The Friendship Centre and the B.C. Native Women's Society also offer courses for special interest groups such as long-term unemployed Native people who are seeking job skills.

All these institutions work with some understanding of the

context of the student's cultural background. The students' experiences with education as a result of this background often provide a starting point for needed skill development in the area of choice. Native administrators from several of these programs have been meeting on a regular basis to discuss the possibilities of establishing a Native-run college in British Columbia.

The list of activities and accomplishments in Native education since the closure of the residential schools, and the subsequent lack of success of many Native students in integration into the public schools, goes on. It is tempting to say, as the Department of Indian Affairs is wont to do, that the future holds nothing but success. But the changes must be examined critically. None has been accomplished easily; all have been the subject of endless analysis and on-going reform. While gaining control of some funding for education is in itself a major step, it cannot compare to the work which must follow. Taking over an entire education system is a long-term process. For Native people, many of whom have had some of the worst schooling experiences imaginable, the task is even more formidable.

While Indian control of Indian education has been an important rallying point for over a decade, the time has come for a critical analysis of the ideas which this phrase holds. Indian control and education have become 'amoeba' words encompassing a realm of meanings and intents. A return to the notion of local control may hold much of the direction intended in the National Indian Brotherhood's original document. Too often, particularly amongst B.C.'s diverse cultures, centralized control has eroded some of the recognition of the differences which are integral to the notion of local control. For some, Indian control stresses that traditional Native values of a specific culture area are of paramount importance. For many, the language holds all. Frequently, 'having a school' is an integral part of Indian control. For some, Indian control appears to mean that a person of Native ancestry can do no wrong. Ultimately, those who find themselves in positions of control may want to take the time to separate themselves from the models of domination and control which have pervaded Native education since the first missionary stopped the first Native child from speaking a Native language. Considering alternatives to residential schools, federally administered day schools, and the public school system is an important part of taking control.

The choice of appropriate models is a decision for the people. Having for too long been the objects of top-down decision making, Native people who rise to positions of power may want to examine very closely the methods which they use for determining the will of the people. They may want to re-consider critically at all stages of their authority the meaning of Indian control of Indian education, for the people with whom and for whom they work. There can be, of course, no single definition—only a constantly renegotiated one arrived at by people engaged in dialogue and mutual action.

What of the other actors in this scenario—the government and the missionaries? How have their roles evolved since the closure of the residential schools? The Department of Indian Affairs continues to control the dollars for Native education throughout the country. In B.C., the Master Tuition Agreement has been the subject of much discontent since the early sixties. It enables the federal and provincial governments and local school districts to negotiate money earmarked for Native students with no involvement of Native people themselves. The human aspects of education are replaced by mere commodities, mythical dollars passing from the hands of one bureaucrat to another. The current agreement was suspended in 1986. The new agreement may include an opting out clause so that bands which are willing and able to control their own negotiations for their children's education may do so.

For these bands, the involvement of the D.I.A. in education will be greatly reduced. They will be able to decide whether to buy services from the local school district, to operate an independent school, or to consider other options such as private schools. One would anticipate that when the financial arrangements are made at the local level, all the parties involved will be close enough to the faces of students who are their friends and relatives, to act with the immediate understanding that their decisions will determine these students' futures.

A major concern of many bands today is the reduction in dollars available for post-secondary students. At a time when more students are returning to school as adults, the amount of money available has become limited. Some students who need extra preparation for success at college and university may find themselves without financial assistance from their bands as the Department of Indian Affairs changes its funding priorities.

Students are already expressing concern about band acceptance of D.I.A. requirements regarding issues such as daycare for the children of students. One person responded strongly to her band's request that she involve a provincial agency in daycare. To that time daycare had been the responsibility of her band. She advocated caution in complying with D.I.A. policy guidelines before consultation with band members. Her letter included the following comments:

> We now have a chief and council governing our affairs; let us have them take control under the direction of our people, not under the direction of D.I.A. . . . . Our government, not the provincial government, should be in control of child care. (MYERS, 1987)

Clearly, this person is seeking a consultative form of government for her band, and is dissatisfied with some band officials' apparently unquestioning compliance with D.I.A. regulations. While some Native people have joined the ranks of the Department of Indian Affairs and may be trying to change the system from within, others feel that only a system which is locally based and which effectively addresses local concerns can improve the relationship of individual bands with the federal government.

The Catholic Church continues to play a major role in the lives of many Native people, particularly those of the residential school generations. In the Kamloops area, the Oblates still serve the people in outlying reserves. While their impact is considerably less than it has been in the past, for many people Catholicism remains a strong influence. Native leaders generally comment very little publicly on the Church, probably out of respect for the commitment of their elders to this form of spirituality.

Some Native people have managed to meld their Catholicism with an awareness of the importance of Native spirituality in their lives. As one Native woman commented: "First I'm an Indian, then I'm a mother, then I'm a wife and, after that, I'm a Catholic" (Mary, personal conversation, August 1987). She has also made many references to the importance of dreaming in her life, a significant aspect of Native spirituality. For other Native people, Catholicism became a subject to avoid. Too many bad experiences outweighed any positive aspects of the religion. Some people have sought religion in other churches, such as Baptist and Pentecostal. Others have returned to Native spiritualism: a few to the traditional spirituality of their own culture and many more to a pan-Indian religious movement which emphasizes aspects of spirituality common to many North American Native cultures. For other Native people, as for many in the general population, religion has become insignificant.

At times, even within families, these diverse beliefs can lead to tension. At a family gathering, the parents may still hold to Catholicism while one grown child may have chosen an evangelical Christian religion and another Native spirituality. One Native woman related a particularly poignant story about the religious clashes within her family. After her father's death, her mother was despondent and it was decided that her husband had taken her soul with him because he did not want to leave her. The mother consulted a traditional medicine woman who sang over her. After the ceremony, the bereaved woman was much relieved. Later, one of her daughters, a born-again Christian, reprimanded her mother, saying that medicine women did the work of the devil. Her son, a practicing Catholic, suggested that she should just go to Church for solace. The tension in the family mounted as the mother expressed confusion and distress in response to her children's reprimands. Another daughter listened in silence, but when the opportunity arose, offered strong support for her mother's traditional spirituality.

On the Kamloops reserve, the church has been restored as a heritage site. It has taken the place of the chapel in the residential school, which was the major gathering place for several decades after the church fell into disrepair. Mass is held in the church on important occasions, but those who attend regularly must cross the river to town. On reserves such as ChuChua and Chase in the area surrounding Kamloops, Oblates still work on a missionary basis. Church involvement in major ceremonies such as weddings and funerals is of continuing importance. A chief in the Kamloops area who is very politically involved, but for whom religion holds little personal relevance, commented on the Church's commitment to the area. He suggested that he would like to see a liberation theologist who would work with the people for social changes as well as for their spiritual needs.

The residential schools themselves are closed. With the exception of one Catholic boarding school primarily attended by Native students in Prince George called Prince George College, there are no schools in the province which bear any resemblance to those which had such tremendous impact on the lives of so many Native people in this province. But the impact goes on. The experiences which are documented in this book continue to affect the lives of the people who lived them. Throughout this province and the country, thousands of Native people carry such stories in their hearts and minds. These are the stories that attest to the strength and perseverance of Native cultures in Canada. These are the stories that must be told to all our children and grandchildren so that they too can come to recognize and appreciate the history of the people who came before them and the power of their legacy of survival.

APPENDIX A
PROBLEM AND LITERATURE REVIEW

"Every time I hear a white person talking about Indians, I get knots in my stomach."
Verna Kirkness
Director of Native Education
University of British Columbia

Antidialogical action, action which is based on the desire of one group in society to dominate and control another group through silencing that group, is a focal point of Paulo Freire's pedagogical theory. His notion of cultural invasion is of a phenomenon in which:

> . . . the invaders penetrate the cultural context of another group, in disrespect of the latter's potentialities; they impose their own view of the world upon those they invade and inhibit the creativity of the invaded by curbing their expression. (1970: 150)

Education, particularly as seen in the residential schools, developed by immigrant Europeans and their descendants for Native people in Canada, has typically been an expression of cultural invasion. As authors of and actors in the invasion, members of the dominating society have attempted to mold and have chosen and acted for Native people who as objects of the invasion were expected to follow the choices made for them. Freire goes on to point out that this kind of domination is perpetrated through invasion whether overt and physical or camouflaged with the invader in the role of the helping friend.

An examination of the experiences of the students who attended the Kamloops Indian Residential School reveals the antidialogical nature of the policies which were designed to control their lives. The school experiences which resulted from these governmental and ecclesiastical policies most often proved to be of dubious or negative value for the Native children who attended the institution. In almost all cases, it was less successful than anticipated by policy makers, teachers, and parents alike.

Although similar notions have been examined previously in literature, particularly in recent decades, little of the writing has involved the actual experiences of Native people. Rather, researchers have consulted archival material: letters and diaries written by Europeans about Native people, registers and other reports compiled by Europeans, and reports filed by European church and government officials about Native people. When they did finally begin to work directly with Native people, researchers tended to distill the experiences into tables of figures surrounded by speculative statements.

This failure to include the words of the Native people who have actually experienced the life described in the documents is nothing short of absurd. Residential schools began in British Columbia little more than one hundred years ago. Most closed in the late 1960s. Literally thousands of Native people currently living in the province attended one or another of the schools at some time and have a wealth of information to share.

When students are consulted, a most significant point recurs within their stories. Hardly passive, native people have consistently resisted the onslaught against themselves and their culture. A focus of study for several educational researchers within the past decade has been the notion of cultural production within schools (Apple, 1977, Giroux, 1981). Whenever an oppressive system is set in place, an opportunity for resistance to that system is also created. Paul Willis, in his study of working class youth in an English industrial town (1977), examines the phenomenon of a counter-school culture:

> Opposition to the school is principally manifested in the struggle to win symbolic and physical space from the institution and its rules. (260)

This resistance to an oppressive system is paralleled in the Kamloops residential school. In the stories, many of the responses of Native children and their parents demonstrate clear defiance of authority, which in turn created a strong support group amongst the students. This community spirit not only permitted, but actually fostered the survival of a strong Native identity, which was perceived by the students themselves as very different from that of the Europeans who served as teachers and supervisors.

Although the residential school indubitably had enormous impact on the lives of all who attended, it failed in its efforts to assimilate Native people into European mainstream society. In the words of the great Shuswap leader, George Manuel:

> At this point in our struggle for survival, the Indian peoples of North America are entitled to declare a victory. We have survived. (1974: 4)

An examination of residential schools from the perspectives of Native people is long overdue. For the children, it has become a necessity. In its historic document entitled *Indian Control of Indian Education*, the National Indian Brotherhood has this to say:

> Unless a child learns about the forces which shape him: the history of his people, their values and customs, their language, he will never really know himself or his potential as a human being. (9)

Within the stories in this study, a people—sometimes disheartened but rarely despairing—fight to retain their values and customs, and their language, and to present their views of a history long disregarded.

LITERATURE REVIEW

In a survey of the literature relevant to a study of the Kamloops Indian Residential School, three areas require consideration. Historical, anthropological, and educational studies all enlighten such a review. Although the three categories overlap at times, the arbitrary distinctions between them facilitate the necessary examination of a great variety of works.

Historically, economic, political, and cultural systems originating in Europe have played the major roles in the development of Canada as a nation. Robin Fisher *(1977)*, referring to historians writing of British Columbia, states that:

> . . . these historians deal with the Indians only as they respond to the European economic system, accommodating to European demands rather than acting in terms of the priority of their own culture. (xi)

Almost without exception, early works showed European

perceptions of Native cultures as inferior and primitive (*Maclean, 1896, Hill-Tout, 1907*). This strong sense of white superiority accompanied by a tendency to generalize, to subsume the many and varied groupings from across the country or across the province into one amorphous grouping, resulted in a hazy view of Native people (*D.I.A., 1960; Grant, 1984*). Because academics writing of Native history have tended to rely on written records for their research, they present most often the views of the white fur trader, settler, Indian agent and missionary (*Morice, 1906; Cronin, 1960; Hewlett, 1964; Wilson, 1985*). By far the majority of the lengthy quotations are the words of Euro-Canadians; all too rarely is attention given to those of the Native people. Because few Native people have kept written records, interviewing is at times the only means of garnering their perceptions of history. With notable exceptions (*Berger, 1977, 1981; Brody, 1981*), few researchers writing of Native people have taken the time to develop the trusting and understanding relationships necessary for open communication and meaningful interviews. Historical writings about Native people to the present time exhibit a deficiency of primary source material explicating Native perspectives.

Because the nature of their work requires that they spend time with the people whom they study, anthropologists have fared somewhat better in presenting the life experiences of Native people. Although some studies suffer through their attempts to present a comprehensive study of Native cultures across the country (*Jenness 1963*), others such as those of James Teit (*1900, 1909*) are in direct contrast. Fluent in a number of Native languages and married to a member of the Thompson Nation, Teit in his life work with the people of the Interior of B.C., has provided invaluable resources on traditional life styles considered accurate by both Native and Euro-Canadian historians. Years after Teit, Wilson Duff produced a book based on extensive ethnographic work throughout the province. As a result, *The Indian History of British Columbia (1964)* presents for the first time in a publication of a general nature a variety of Native views on the impact of the Europeans on their societies. About the same time, Wax, Wax and Dumont (*1964*) produced a detailed case study of the education of the Oglala Sioux of the Pine Ridge reservation. Thorough field research resulted in a clearly developed study with emphasis on the Native perspective.

This example was followed quickly by a number of case studies *(Wolcott, 1967; King, 1967; Brow, 1967)*. All of these studies are obviously the work of academics involved for only a limited time with the people whom they studied, frequently with a predetermined agenda. Although they do present a personal view of the objects of their study, their understanding could be said to lack the depth which comes with long-term contact. A significant aspect of these studies is the inclusion of a number of lengthy quotations by Native people.

Educational writings, as all writings, are influenced by the society within which they are formed. British Columbia has a history preceding Confederation which refuses to acknowledge the existence of Native people. Unlike other provinces, few treaties dealing with relatively few portions of land were drawn up to address the issue of aboriginal title. Douglas, the first governor of the colony of Vancouver Island, insisted that:

> ... only after the aboriginal title had been extinguished by treaty could settlement proceed ... the settlers denied that it was their responsibility, and they would not vote funds for the purpose. (BERGER, 1981: 222-23)

The policy of denying that aboriginal title had ever existed persisted when the new colony of British Columbia united with Vancouver Island in 1866. Because the provincial government chose to ignore Native people, no consideration was given to their education. The federal government's assumption of responsibility for Native people in 1876 reinforced this attitude. In his 1936 doctoral dissertation, "The History of Education in the Crown Colonies of Vancouver Island and British Columbia and in the Province of British Columbia," Donald MacLaurin, the Assistant Superintendant of Education for B.C., does not even mention Native people. As a result of federal control as outlined in the Indian Act, people writing about Native education tended to write about it as a national concern. Reports and research often failed to consider the concerns or perspectives of individual tribal nations, but rather reflected the national views of the Department of Indian Affairs.

Much of the research and publishing on Native education has been done under the auspices of the Department of Indian Affairs (DIA). Materials which embellish the department's image and depict its successes are more acceptable than those which might lead to suggestions of racism and ultimately threaten the careers of the elected officials at its head. A book entitled *The Education of Indian Children in Canada (1965)* presents itself as "A symposium written by members of the Indian Affairs Education Division with Comments by the Indian Peoples." It outlines policy decisions and changing legislation. The direct involvement of Native people is found only in the short commentaries which follow each chapter.

On the topic of Native involvement in decision-making, the closing chapter contains a most revealing statement.

> At present the education of Indian people is directed almost exclusively by outsiders. The federal, provincial and municipal authorities argue, discuss and decide. Indian people participate , but more to ratify than to plan, so is it any wonder that Indians continue to remain unexcited about our program for their education? (INDIAN AFFAIRS EDUCATION DIVISION, 1965: 96)

This paradoxical approach continues to the present day: while paying lip-service to involvement of the people in self-determination, those in control simultaneously present plans for ratification. In Freire's words,

> The invaders act; those they invade have only the illusion of action, through the action of the invaders. (1977: 150)

The Hawthorn report *(1967)*, while generalizing as *A Survey of the Contemporary Indians of Canada*, is structured around research with a number of bands across the country. As is the case with many of the historical writings, the credited quotations are those of the white experts: church people, school people, and department people. Generally limited to single words and phrases, Native people's responses to questions regarding the need for education are made to sound shallow and ill-conceived: "Education makes life easier," or "Education helps you get along with whites better." *(Hawthorn, 1967: 137)*. The Indian voices are given only through layers of European interpreters.

Few works on residential schools in western Canada exist. *The School at Mopass (King, 1967)*, a study of a Yukon residential school, is thorough and includes considerable comment on the school by Native students and workers. The study was commissioned by the Indian Affairs Branch because officials found that the school:

. . . is dysfunctional in the sense that it does not produce the kind of product which it is intended to produce. The desired 'product' might be defined as a well-integrated Canadian citizen equipped with attitudes and intellectual skills that enable him to function within the larger society in basically the same manner as other citizens. (ix)

Despite the author's intent not to be influenced by the sponsorship of his study, his ethnocentric bias surfaces in comments such as:

Those elements [of traditional culture] that linger seem to be a reactive defense mechanism for coping with the powerful but generally apathetic Whiteman society rather than a deliberate or functional persistence of cultural traits as valued entities in themselves. (27)

On the other hand, his criticisms of the school and nearly all portions of society responsible for its inhumanity and ineffectiveness are well-taken.

Two articles published separately in *BC Studies* include some interesting insights into residential schools. Coates *(1985)*, relies heavily on archival material, including files of letters from Native people to school officials, to construct his thesis that the school at Carcross in the Yukon " . . . failed to provide the Native students with an obvious route into either native or white society." *(47)* Redford *(1980)* summarizes attendance statistics to demonstrate the control which Native parents had over the starting date and the duration of their children's time at residential school. A recent collection of articles entitled *Indian Education in Canada (Barman et al, 1986)* includes several allusions to residential schools in Canada. Although the emphasis is on archival material as a source of data, it includes notable exceptions such as the linguistic study of Battiste and the summary of an extensive study by Persson *(1980)* on the Blue Quills school in Northern Alberta.

Other references to residential schools are found within larger studies. Mary Ashworth *(1979)* took the time to interview a former residential school student for inclusion as a part of a chapter on the history of Native education in B.C. Her use of other Native sources for her information led her to the conclusion that Native people must control their own education, an indication of the depth of her understanding of the current situation in Native education.

In summary, three points regarding existing writings about Native people are paramount. Although archival material, particularly primary sources which may include the recording of Native comments, is worthwhile in examining history from a Native perspective, only careful interpretation can expose the Euro-Canadian bias of much of the material. Whenever possible, archival material should serve only as a starting point for research about Native people, and should be complemented with information gathered in interviews. Because of the relatively short duration of the Euro-Canadian presence in B.C., there are still many older Native people who have a wealth of memories to contribute to an effort at understanding their perspectives of events which may be documented only minimally in the various archives. Finally, few detailed studies have been conducted on the Native experience in residential schools. None exists for the Kamloops Indian Residential School prior to the current study.

APPENDIX B
METHODOLOGY

"don't rhyme the words too closely
when you tell our story
leave time and space for us to install
our bit of truth . . . . "

Sheila Erickson
(in *Gooderham*, 1972: 40)

The analysis of the methodology used for collecting and presenting this research falls into two major sections. Part one includes the reasons for using certain methods. The second section recounts details of the methods themselves, i.e., how the research was conducted and how the data was selected for presentation.

THE REASONS

Understanding human experience is the central task of the educational researcher . . . . Too often, theory fails to speak to the personal everyday life-worlds of the students and becomes instead another set of alienating constructs. (POLAKOW, 1985: 826)

Valerie Polakow, in a recent article, elaborates on the importance of storytelling in developing theory concerning those groups in society who have tended to remain voiceless—the invaded and the oppressed. The article points out that too much of modern educational research has been an attempt to emulate the so-called true sciences.

In contemporary social science, stories are soft—they do not constitute the real data of the scientific enterprise . . . The isolation of body, of mind, of experience, of consciousness leads to documentation, to a mere taxonomy of facts closed in on themselves, leading us away from, not towards, the understanding of human experience. (POLAKOW: 826)

Decrying this approach to research, she goes on to point out the importance of storytelling as a form of research. The careful selection of stories by the researcher who " . . . is an embedded participant, not a distant, uninvolved observer of the human-scope . . . . " *(Polakow: 826)* provides the key to storytelling as human science research. In works cited earlier, such as those of George Manuel and James Teit, the writers have indeed taken the time to live the lives whereof they write.

I began the formal research for this study of the Kamloops Indian Residential School as an informal participant observer involved in 'the process of living'. My involvement with Native people in the Kamloops area spans a period of fifteen years. Originally, as a teacher in two of the secondary schools, I worked with some Native students in my classes. Another in-tense connection was through a rodeo company in which I played an active role. A number of Native people in the Kamloops area have lifetime commitments to rodeo. Over the years I developed strong friendships with some of the rodeo people. Twelve years ago, in 1976, I moved into the field of Native education through my work as co-ordinator of the Native Indian Teacher Education Program, an alternative program offered by the University of British Columbia for prospective elementary teachers. In this capacity, I served as teacher, coun-sellor, seminar leader, and practicum supervisor working with Native adults. I mention these involvements because they have provided the basis for long term trusting relationships with people. The friendships served as the starting point which, when accompanied by an explanation of the work which I was doing, enabled me to talk with the people in depth about an emotion-filled area. As my knowledge of the Native people's lives and history grew, the importance and lack of documenta-tion of the impact of the residential school became clearer to me. The interviews provided an opportunity to focus on what had emerged as an area of concern and significance for many Native people of the Kamloops area.

Only with the direct involvement—the words—of the people in the presentation of history can one approach a Native per-spective. Through these words, the residential school which lives in the memories of the participants takes shape before our eyes. The cultural invasion and the resistance to this invasion and ultimately the survival and persistence of a group of people in the central Interior of British Columbia become the emphases of this book.

A strong sense of irony focussed my attention on the stories of the students of K.I.R.S. Originally the senior girls' dormitory, the top floor of the east side of the huge brick building completed in 1923 now houses a program for Native people who wish to become elementary teachers. Frequently, students coming to be interviewed for admission or to class for the first time said very calmly, "My bed was right by that window . . . " or that door, or around that corner. With only slight encouragement, the stories began to pour forth—stories of loneliness, pain, camaraderie, and resilience. The irony of the situation comes with the people who have returned to a place of their youth, a place of what was often very difficult formal education, to study to be teachers. They come by choice, as mature students, with clear goals in mind. How different from the other times.

The Kamloops Indian Band owns the buildings which were until recently the Kamloops Indian Residential School. As I have discussed earlier, within these buildings, educational activities from historical research to curriculum development are in progress. They have the potential to affect and have already affected the school lives of the band children. In order to appreciate this phenomenon as a tremendous expression of the survival of a culture and a group of people, I felt it necessary to delve into the history which has led to this present state. Beneath the current surge in educational activity lies almost a century of formal education for the most part dominated and controlled by religious and governmental policies established unilaterally by European society.

THE METHODS

Initially, my formal research relies heavily on written material to present something of the attitudes and ambitions which guided those people who established and controlled the residential school. Records at the Public Archives of British Columbia, Oblate House in Vancouver, the Secwepemc Museum and Archives, and the libraries at Cariboo College and the University of B.C. provided a brief but basic picture of the European perspective. That total cultural annihilation was the goal of government and missionaries is undeniable when one examines the written records. That these efforts to assimilate Native people were on the whole successfully resisted is the ultimate focus of the preceding stories.

Because the stories of the people so vividly depict life in the residential school, frequently in a very different light than that which the written records suggest, interviewing was deemed the most satisfactory approach to presenting some of the history of the school from a Native perspective. Thirteen intensive one to two hour interviews form the kernel of the data. In addition, I have kept field notes on more casual discussions with numerous other Native people.

Interviews were taped and transcribed. Because two participants did not want to be taped, I made notes during the interviews. I was particularly interested in facets of school life which were deemed contrary to values and beliefs held before coming to school; in the forms of resistance which students developed to the foreign expectations of the people in charge; and finally, in the effects which schooling had on the students' relationships with their families when they returned home.

The interviews themselves were very flexible. Although I prepared a schedule (see *Appendix D*), I rarely referred to it during an interview. Instead the direction of the interview was determined by the stories the person wanted to tell. At times, the flow of the interview was guided more by the stories which the person had to tell than by my schedule. Without exception, the issues of cultural violation and resistance to that violation were mentioned. The place of interviewing was most often my office which was located in the residential school buildings. The room itself stirred many memories: "This used to be sister's bedroom," commented one participant. On some occasions, particularly when speaking with older people, I went to their homes. My kitchen table was also the site of many tales told by casual visitors about the residential school.

Generally I chose to interview people with whom I had already had contact or people whom others had suggested as strong participants. Those who hesitated when I asked them, I did not interview. Throughout the interview, people were made aware that they could end it whenever they chose, and that they could refuse to answer any questions. Almost without exception, people spoke most openly and informatively about their school lives. Needless to say, the interviewing which I did only scratched the surface. Many important stories are still unrecorded.

Because of the intense emotions involved in sharing pieces of life with an interviewer, one must have established a warm relationship before the interview, or be capable of establishing rapport quickly. In a cross-cultural situation, this ability is crucial, as is some awareness of specific cultural interaction patterns. I do not mean to imply in any way that this relationship should be developed in an exploitive way, in order to interview, but rather the converse. The accounts reproduced here were generally fuller and more open than is often the case with one-time interviews, for the most part because of a long term relationship between the interviewer and the participant.

Two of the main problems with interviewing, particularly in asking people to recall events which are in the distant past, are the selectivity of memory and the possible distortion of these memories over time. I would like to present for consideration two points in this regard. Selection of material presented is a problem encountered with any documentation of fact or history. Memories which survive over time in people's minds are usually those of the more salient experiences. Rather than seeing time as distorting, we might consider it as a filter which allows clearer vision of the matters of importance in a person's life.

Secondly, I feel it is essential to emphasize the oral tradition of the Shuswap people and aboriginal people of the surrounding regions. Unlike some Native cultures in Canada, those in the central Interior of the province did not traditionally transmit culture in written form. As has already been mentioned, storytelling has been the most important means of passing along history and traditions. Even in the now literate culture of the Shuswap, the ability to tell stories with accuracy is respected as a skill. Storytelling, often in the guise of entertainment, continues to be an important dialogical tool for passing along truths. I propose that the long tradition of storytelling—one which includes the re-telling of stories many times with little or no change (Teit, 1909: 621)—contributes to accurate presentation of events even long after their occurrence. One participant commented on this notion as it exists in her culture: "There is no distinction between telling lies and not remembering or exaggerating. There's no difference; all of them are lies" *(Nancy: 4)*. For this person, remembering is a value-laden activity. Closely associated with telling the truth, speaking remembrances is socially acceptable only when it is faithful to the previous accounts.

As my interviewing progressed, I found my mental image of the school constantly changing. Each new idea expressed produced a slight reshuffling of the pieces which made up the visualization which I was developing of the school. Occasionally an interview produced so many ideas or an idea of such import, it was as if in turning a kaleidoscope, the overall pattern changed radically, incorporating the old bits of coloured glass with new bits to form an entirely new design. These inital reactions to the interviews were followed by the more comprehensive analysis of the transcriptions of the interviews and a review of the field notes.

The deeper analysis began with a thorough reading of the transcripts. At that time, I marked noteworthy points. On a second reading, I prepared a list of the most striking topics which arose from each interview. These consisted of points which I felt would be useful in re-creating the participants' perspectives of the school and its effects on them. I had in my mind a general direction in which the information might lead me, but remained open to changes which secondary examination of the data might encourage me to emphasize. I found myself thinking most often of a quiltmaker. The people I talked with created the squares and my job was to arrange them in an effective design and to stitch them together to fashion an impressive entity. The stories form our quilt, made of people's strength, resistance, pain, change and adaptation.

In an effort to maintain the confidentiality of the interviews, I have included only minimal details about each person. I have assigned each study participant a pseudonym and a number and have included the following details: tribal origin, year of birth, and years of attendance at the school (see *Appendix C*). The presentation of the data for the most part is not arranged chronologically. When I felt that the time of a particular comment was important, I have usually indicated a decade. Although many policies changed over the term of the school's operation, outstanding is the commonality of feeling about the school. Some details of daily life changed with the policy, but the study participants' attitudes to an oppressive and dehumanizing system remained fairly constant.

Because I came to the Native culture as a privileged guest, I felt that it was most important to seek the people's approval of my work before beginning it. The recently formed Secwepemc Cultural Education Society has as its mandate " . . . to work in unity to: Preserve and Record—Perpetuate and Enhance our Shuswap Language, History and Culture" *(Secwepemc Cultural Education Society, 1982)*. Because non-Native people in general and academics in particular have often been rightfully accused of approaching Native culture and experience in an insensitive and exploitive way, I wanted to address this concern directly. With the society's approval and working closely with staff and some board members of the society, I felt more confident that my work would not simply be an ethnocentric academic exercise, but that it might prove useful and enlightening to the Shuswap in the work for positive education for their people. I also felt it was important to give the participants an opportunity to comment on my use of their stories and my speculations regarding what they had shared. I met with the majority of them following the writing of this, and without exception, they approved of what I had written and the way in which I had edited their words.

APPENDIX C
PARTICIPANTS

Pseudonyms	Birthdate	Attendance
1. Cecilia		
Female, Shuswap	b. 1900(?)	1907-1908
2. Martha		
Female, Shuswap	b. 1918(?)	1927-1930
3. Sophie		
Female, Shuswap	b. 1918	1926-1934
4. Leo		
Male, Shuswap	b. 1924	1930-1940
5. Josephine		
Female, Shuswap	b. 1925(?)	1935-1944
6. Charlie		
Male, Shuswap	b. 1929	1938-1950
7. Mary		
Female, Shuswap	b. 1931	1940-1951
8. Anne		
Female, Shuswap	b. 1942	1959
9. Neil		
Male, Shuswap	b. 1944	1952-1960
10. Linda		
Female, Lillooet	b. 1947	1952-1960
11. Sam		
Male, Shuswap	b. 1947	1958-1961
12. Alice		
Female, Thompson	b. 1950	1957-1963
13. Nancy		
Female, Chilcotin	b. 1957	1965-1967

APPENDIX D
INTERVIEW SCHEDULE

1. Tell me about your involvement with the school. Years? Grades?
2. What were the rules which stood out in your mind?
3. Children often have ways of getting around rules. Did you? Did others? In what ways?
4. Describe your day. What did you do in the classroom? What subjects? How long? Specific lessons?
5. How often did you go home? Where was it? Did your parents visit? Describe visits.
6. Were there aspects of school which contradicted what you were taught at home? What were they?
7. Religion was an important part of school. Was it compatible with what you had learned at home?
8. And friends. Did you see friends resisting school? Complying with school?
9. Going home. How was it to go home? Were there adjustments within yourself that had to be made? Did friends or other relatives struggle with going home?

MAP OF BANDS OF
SHUSWAP NATION

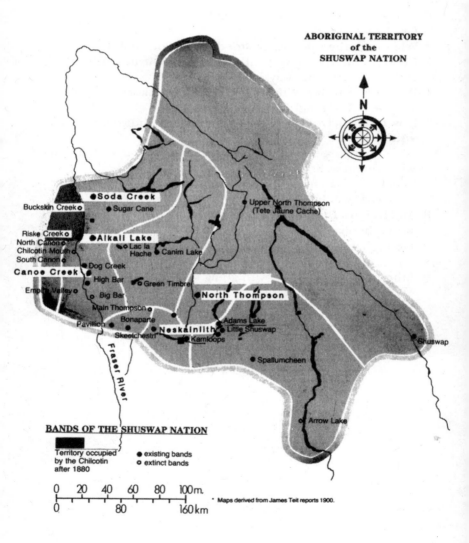

ABORIGINAL TERRITORY
of the
SHUSWAP NATION

N

Soda Creek

Buckskin Creek○

● Sugar Cane

Upper North Thompson
(Tete Jaune Cache)

Riske Creek○
North Canon○
Chilcotin Mouth○
South Canon○

Alkali Lake

○ Lac la
Hache   ● Canim Lake

Canoe Creek

● Dog Creek

Empire Valley○

● High Bar

○ Green Timber

● Big Bar

North Thompson

○ Main Thompson

Pavillion

● Bonaparte

Adams Lake
Little Shuswap

Skeelchestn●   ● Neskainlith

Kamloops

Shuswap

● Spallumcheen

Fraser River

○ Arrow Lake

BANDS OF THE SHUSWAP NATION

Territory occupied
by the Chilcotin
after 1880

● existing bands
○ extinct bands

0   20   40   60   80   100 m.
0   80   160 km

* Maps derived from James Teit reports 1900.

158

APPENDIX F
STUDY IMPLICATIONS

"And when the telling is done and the voices of the voiceless are heard, does story-telling not invoke a call to action?"

Valerie Polakow (826)

Paulo Freire writes of the antithesis of cultural invasion as cultural synthesis. Characterized by dialogue amongst the people involved, the notion of cultural sythesis is fluid. The people listen authentically to one another as a basis for action.

> In cultural sythesis the actors who come from 'another world' to the world of the people do so not as invaders. They do not come to *teach* or to *give* anything, but rather to learn with the people about the people's world. (FREIRE, 1970: 181)

Through this learning, people can then begin to work together for a better world for all involved. Contrary to the children's residential school experience, no individual or group holds the power. It becomes the domain of all who learn and act.

This model has been adopted by the liberation theologists of South American and other so-called Third World countries, much to the consternation of the established Catholic church. Contrary to the notion of blind obedience to superiors, these priests take their direction from the people with whom they work. As a direct threat to the established line of authority and its concommitant distribution of power, liberation theologists visualize power lying with the people. The ability to know themselves and to direct the changes in their lives is ultimately power-giving and humanizing.

Educational leaders would be wise to follow such a model *(Witulief, 1985; Quade, 1982)* and to abandon the hierarchical concepts of the past. Educational institutions from teacher training programs to elementary and pre-schools must be responsive to local experiences and needs. Teachers must design their lessons with the knowledge of their students' lives as well as the subject matter more often deemed important. The opportunity

159

for students and their families to play an active role in their learning both in school and out must be integral to any successful education system. Freire's pedagogical model, in direct contrast to the banking method of education exemplified by the residential school, demands thoughtful action on the part of all involved in the education system. This praxis is both humanizing and liberating.

In light of the residential school experience, the necessity of adopting a similar model in government and its instituions must be addressed. Only through the people and the elected officials recognizing their power and working together in dialogue can meaningful change come about. Within the education system, Native people have effected change through insistence on dialogue. Andrew Paull's strong statements in 1946 and those of the National Indian Brotherhood in 1973 had effect. The system must be restructured to welcome such input as a part of meaningful dialogue rather than forcing confrontational reactions through their inability to include authentic consultation with Native people.

The strength of Native culture is evident in the way Native people dealt with the institution of residential school by successfully resisting its interventions in their lives. Repelling its goal of assimilation, Native people adopted aspects which appeared worthwhile while rejecting others. Those who questioned, who refuused to accept the authoritarian system perpetrated upon them, survived. With the strength of family, of seniors and from within themselves, the survivors refused to comply fully with the oppressors' efforts to dictate their lifestyle. Rather, they adapted the invaders' lifestyle to their own way of being. Catholicism was combined with Native spiritualism; the English language was accepted, but Native languages were never ecompletely abandoned. Traditions and customs passed on through generations were maintained. Native people resisted; Native culture survived; and today the two are rising forces for action and change within a self-defined Native context.

The residential school is closed. The buildings now owned by the Kamloops Indian Band are, as has already been mentioned, the scene of increasing, Native-controlled activity. People can justly celebrate this expression of the indomitable human spirit.

The individuals who participated in this study are all survivors. Although many have experienced and continue to experience the need to put the impact of residential school into perspective, they are at the same time contributing to the continuation of their culture in innumerable ways. As parents and grandparents, teachers and students, politicians and band executives, entrepreneurs and rodeo champions, they define their Native culture in its vibrant and evolutionary state.

Implications for further research revealed by this study are myriad. More detailed studies on some of the aspects introduced here could prove most rewarding: the cliques of the 1950s, arranged marriages, Native people who returned to the residential school as workers and teachers, and more extensive study of particular time periods are only a few examples. Related topics include people's perceptions of integration into public schools and the current move to band-operated schools. The whole area of language retention, of what is viewed by some of the participants as temporary language inhibition, and the increasing efforts to re-establish language for those who have had little or no opportunity to learn it, could also prove to be fruitful areas of study.

For those whose goal is to quantify, this study in itself can provide the basis for very meaningful empirical studies. The use of field research, in particular the open-ended interview, can serve as the focus for quantitative analyses of a number of areas touched upon in this work.

Educational and social programs developed partially to enable people to face and deal with the impact of residential school and other aspects of cultural invasion are operating in the Kamloops area. In direct contrast to the oppressive system described in these pages, the programs build upon an examination of cultural identity and an appreciation of self as a basis for meaningful education in any subject area. Programs such as Native Human Services, K.E.E.N., a re-entry program operated by the B.C. Native Women's Society, and the college preparation course developed by the Interior Salishan Education Council and the Secwepemc Cultural Education Society are areas for thought-provoking research. Their integration of traditional values and culturally appropriate methods with necessary content are another facet of the process which has enabled Native people to survive and grow during the first 200 years of contact with Euro-Canadians. These distinctive approaches hold possible implications for other Native education programs and any humanizing pedagogy.

The substance of this study also holds implications for academics and researchers who address Native issues. Listening and learning must form the basis for cross-cultural research. For too long, Euro-Canadians have studied documents written by other Euro-Canadians about Native people as the basis for analysis of Native culture. Archives may serve as an aid to understanding the history of a culture, but in all research the people who proceed from that history should be directly involved in the researcher's work in some way. To understand a people's history, a learner should start with the living generation of that culture. Their combined life experiences most often bring them closer to their history than any book or paper in a library can. Not only the basis for educational developments, dialogue should serve as the groundwork for research as well. The people and the academics must work together in data gathering, in analyzing data, and ultimately in building authentic theory.

Acceptance of all people's experience as legitimate and the sharing of perceptions and biases in true efforts to arrive at common understanding create the possibility for fruitful action. In the words of Rita Jack, the administrator of the Secwepemc Cultural Education Society,

> The legacy of the residential school experience is that we now have genrations of Shuswap people who, not by their own choice, are unable to participate in the academic education of their children.
>
> In order to best plan for the future educational needs of Shuswap children, it is necessary to acknowledge the present situation . . . . We need once more to make education a priority in communities. (1985: 9)

With an understanding of the past, people can participate in dialogue with one another to make a different future. The strength which resisted the onslaught of cultural invasion perpetrated by the residential school for almost a century is the strength of a people and a culture which continues to survive and grow.

BIBLIOGRAPHY

Acts of Visitation. Kamloops Indian Residential School 1943-1966. Oblate Archives, Vancouver, B.C.

Adams, David W. "Before Canada: Toward an Ethnohistory of Indian Education." *History of Education Quarterly.* Vol. 28, No. 1, Spring 1988.

Angus, Mary, Ann Paul and Karen Thomas. *The Summer Student Project: Ren Kye 7e (My Grandmother).* Kamloops: B.C. Native Women's Society, 1983.

Anonymous. *Letter*, Ottawa: 21 March 1908. PABC RG 10 Vol. 6001 File 1-1-1 Pt. 2 School Files.

Apple, Michael. "Social Structure, Ideology and Curriculum" in Martin Lawn & Len Barton, eds. *Rethinking Curriculum Studies: A Radical Approach.* London: Croom Helm, 1981.

Archibald, Jo-ann. "Locally Developed Native Studies Curriculum: An Historical and Philosophical Rationale." Presented to the International Conference of the Mokakit Indian Education Research Association. London: University of Western Ontario, 1984.

Ashworth, Mary. *The Forces Which Shaped Them.* Vancouver: New Star Books, 1979.

Barman, Jean, Yvonne Hebert, and Don McCaskill. *Indian Education in Canada Volume 1: The Legacy.* Vancouver: University of British Columbia Press, 1986.

Barman, Jean, Yvonne Hebert, and Don McCaskill. *Indian Education in Canada, Volume 2: The Challenge.* Vancouver: University of British Columbia Press, 1987.

Becker, Howard S. *Outsiders: Studies in the Sociology of Deviance.* New York: The Free Press, 1963.

——. *Sociological Work: Method and Substance.* New Brunswick, N.J.: Aldine Publishing Company, 1970.

Berger, Thomas. *Fragile Freedoms.* Vancouver: Clarke, Irwin & Co., 1981.

Borg, Walter R. and Meredith Gall. *Educational Research.* New York: Longman, 1979.

Bowd, Alan D. "Ten Years After the Hawthorn Report." *Canadian Psychological Review* 18:4, October 1977.

British Columbia. Royal Commission on Indian Affairs. Evidence submitted to the Royal Commission. Kamloops Agency, 1913.

Brody, Hugh. *Maps and Dreams.* Vancouver: Douglas & McIntyre, 1981.

Brow, Catherine Judith. "A Socio-cultural History of the Alkali Lake Shuswap, 1882-1966." Thesis. University of Washington, 1967.

Canadian Education Association. *Recent Developments in Native Education.* Toronto, 1984.

Cardinal, Harold. *The Rebirth of Canada's Indians.* Edmonton: Hurtig Publishers, 1977.

Coates, Kenneth. " 'Betwixt and Between': The Anglican Church and the Children of Carcross (Chooutla) Residential School, 1911-1954." *B.C. Studies*. Vol. 64, Winter 1985.

Creighton, Donald. Canada: *The Heroic Beginnings*. Toronto: Macmillan of Canada, 1974.

Cronin, Kay. *Cross in the Wilderness*. Vancouver: Mitchell Press, 1960.

Davin, Nicholas F. *Report on Industrial Schools for Indians and Halfbreeds*. Ottawa: 14 March 1879. PABC RG 10 Vol. 6001 File 1-1-1, Pt. 1.

Dawson, George. *Notes on the Shuswap People of British Columbia*. Transactions of the Royal Society of Canada, 1891.

Department of Citizenship and Immigration Indian Affairs Branch. *Indians of British Columbia (An Historical Review)*. Ottawa: Indian Affairs Branch, 1960.

Duff, Wilson. *The Indian History of British Columbia*. Victoria: Provincial Museum of Natural History and Anthropology, 1964.

Fisher, Robin. *Contact and Conflict*. Vancouver: University of British Columbia Press, 1977.

Freire, Paulo. *Pedagogy of the Oppressed*. New York: Continuum, 1970.

Fulton, Hilary J.M. *The Melting Snowman: The Canadian Indian Residence as a Place for Children to Live and Grow*. Ottawa: D.I.A.N.D., 1972.

Gibellini, Rosino, ed. *Frontiers of Theology in Latin America*. Maryknoll: Orbis Books, 1979.

Giroux, Henry A. *Ideology, Culture and the Process of Schooling*. Philadelphia: Temple University Press, 1981.

Gooderham, Kent, ed. *I Am An Indian*. Toronto: J.M. Dent and Sons, 1969.

——. *Notice This Is an Indian Reserve*. Toronto: Griffin House, 1972.

Gresko, Jacqueline (Kennedy). "Roman Catholic Missionary Effort and Indian Acculturation in the Fraser Valley, B.C. 1860-1900." Unpublished B.A. Honours Essay, University of British Columbia, 1969.

——. "White 'Rites' and Indian 'Rites': Indian Education and Native Responses in the West, 1870-1910." In Jones, Stamp and Sheehan, eds. *Shaping the Schools of the Canadian West*. Calgary: Detselig, 1979.

——. "Creating Little Dominions within the Dominion: Early Catholic Indian Schools in Saskatchewan and British Columbia." In Barman et al. *Indian Education in Canada, Vol. 1. The Legacy*. Vancouver: University of British Columbia Press, 1986.

Hawthorn, H.B. *A Survey of the Contemporary Indians of Canada Vol. II*. Ottawa: Queen's Printer, 1967.

Hewlett, Edward S. "The Chilcotin Uprising: A Study of Indian-White Relations in Nineteenth Century British Columbia." Thesis. Vancouver: University of British Columbia, 1964.

Hill-Tout, C. *British North America I. The Far West: The Home of the Salish and Dene*. London: Archibald Constable and Co., 1907.

Indian Act. Ottawa: Queen's Printer, 1978.

Indian Affairs Branch and University of British Columbia Extension Department. *Proceedings of the Conference on the Indian Child and His Education*. Vancouver: University of British Columbia Extension Department, 1967.

Indian Affairs Education Division. *The Education of Indian Children in Canada*. Toronto: Ryerson Press, 1965.

Jack, Rita. "Legacy of the Indian Residential School." *Secwepemc Cultural Arts Magazine*. Vol.1, No.1.

Jenness, Diamond. *The Indians of Canada*. Ottawa: Information Canada, 1963.

Kamloops Souvenir Edition. Kamloops Indian Residential School. May 21, 1977. Secwepemc Cultural Education Society.

King, A. Richard. *The School at Mopass: A Problem Of Identity*. Toronto: Holt, Rinehart and Winston, 1967.

Kirk, Ruth. *Wisdom of the Elders*. Vancouver: Douglas & McIntyre in association with the B.C. Provincial Museum, 1986.

Kleinfeld, Judith. "Effective Teachers of Eskimo and Indian Students." *School Review*, February 1975.

Kirkness, Verna J. *Evaluation Report of Indians in Federal and Provincial Schools in Manitoba*. Ottawa: Department of Indian Affairs and Northern Development, 1978.

——. "The Education of Canadian Indian Children," *Child Welfare*. LX:7, July-August 1981.

——. "Indian Teachers—A Key to Progress." Address to University of Saskatoon, February 27, 1985.

LaViolette, Forrest E. *The Struggle for Survival: Indian Cultures and the Protestant Ethic in British Columbia*. Toronto: University of Toronto Press, 1973.

Latham, Barbara K. and Roberta J. Pazdro. Not Just Pin Money: Selected Essays on the History of Women's Work in British Columbia. Victoria: Camosun College, 1984.

MacLaurin, Donald. "The History of Education in the Crown Colonies of Vancouver Island and British Columbia and in the Province of British Columbia." Dissertation. University of Washington, 1936.

Maclean, John. *Canadian Savage Folk: The Native Tribes of Canada*. Toronto: William Briggs, 1896.

Mann, Peter H. *Methods of Social Investigation*. New York: Basil Blackwell Ltd., 1968.

Manuel, George and Michael Posluns. *The Fourth World: An Indian Reality*. Toronto: Collier-MacMillan, 1974.

Matthew, Marie. *Introduction to the Shuswap People*. Kamloops: Secwepemc Cultural Education Society, 1986.

McKay, Alvin and Bert McKay. "Education as a Total Way of Life: The Nisga'a Experience." in Barman et al. *Indian Education in Canada: Volume 2, The Challenge*. Vancouver: University of British Columbia Press, 1987.

Merkel, Ray H. "Traditional Indian Education." Unpublished paper of The Traditional Indian Education Society, n.d.

Miller, Kahn-Tineta and George Lerchs. *The Historical Development of the Indian Act*. Ottawa(?): Treaties and Historical Research Branch, P.R.E. Group, Indian and Northern Affairs, 1978.

Morice, A.G. *The History of the Northern Interior of British Columbia*. Smithers: Interior Stationery, 1978.

More, Arthur J. Unpublished paper. Vancouver: University of British Columbia, 1978.

——. *Okanagan Nicola Indian Quality of Education Study*. Penticton: Okanagan Indian Learning Institute, 1984.

Morse, J.J. *"Education Comes to Kamloops." Kamloops Sentinel.* July 11, 1949: 3.

Mulvihill, James. "On Integration," *Tape 130-2*. Kamloops: Secwepemc Cultural Education Society Resource Centre, 1957.

Myers, Maria. Letter to her band. March, 1987.

National Indian Brotherhood. *Indian Control of Indian Education*. Ottawa: National Indian Brotherhood, 1972.

Ormsby, Margaret A. *British Columbia: A History*. Toronto: Macmillan, 1958.

Parminter, A.V. "The Development of Integrated Schooling for British Columbia." Thesis. Vancouver: University of British Columbia, 1964.

Persson, Diane. "The Changing Experience of Indian Residential Schooling: Blue Quills, 1913-1970." In Barman et al. *Indian Education in Canada, Volume 1, The Legacy*. Vancouver: University of British Columbia Press, 1986.

——. "Blue Quills: A Case Study of Indian Residential Schooling." Ph.D. Dissertation. University of Alberta, 1980.

Peterson, L.R. "Indian Education in British Columbia." Thesis. Vancouver: University of British Columbia, 1959.

Polakow, Valerie. "Whose Stories Should We Tell? A Call to Action." *Language Arts 62:8*. December, 1985.

Prentice, Alison L. and Susan E. Houston. *Family, School and Society In Nineteenth-Century Canada*. Toronto: Oxford University Press, 1975.

Quade, Quentin, ed. *The Pope and Revolution*. Washington, D.C.: Ethics and Public Policy Center, 1982.

Redford, James. "Attendance at Indian Residential Schools In British Columbia, 1890-1920." *B.C. Studies* No. 44, Winter 1979-80.

Saintonge, L.N. *Letter to Father LeJeune*. Troy, New York, 19 June 1892. Kamloops: SCES Vertical File: Father LeJeune.

Secwepemc Cultural Arts Magazine. 1:1 June, 1985.

Secwepemc Cultural Education Society. *The Shuswap Declaration*. Kamloops: SCES, 1982.

Special Joint Committee of the Senate and the House of Commons Appointed to Examine and Consider the Indian Act. *Minutes of Proceedings and Evidence* No. 1. Ottawa: King's Printer, 1947.

Stanbury, W.T. *Success and Failure: Indians in Urban Society*. Vancouver: University of British Columbia Press, 1975.

Teit, James. *The Shuswap. 1909*. New York: AMS Press, 1975.

——. *The Thompson Indians of British Columbia. 1900*. New York: AMS Press, 1975.

Titley, Brian. "Duncan Campbell Scott and Indian Education Policy." In

J.D. Wilson, ed. *An Imperfect Past: Education and Society in Canadian History*. Vancouver: University of British Columbia CSCI, 1984.

——. *A Narrow Vision*. Vancouver: University of British Columbia Press, 1986.

Union of B.C. Indian Chiefs. *Claims Based on Native Title*. Vancouver: Union of B.C. Indian Chiefs, 1971.

VanKoughnet, L. *Letter to John A. MacDonald*. Ottawa: 26 August 1887. PABC RG 10 Vol. 6001 File 1-1-1, Pt. 1.

Vayro, Celia. "Enlightened Self-Understanding and Interpretation: Mutual or One Way?" Unpublished. Vancouver, 1987.

Wax, M.L., R.R. Wax, and R.V. Dumont, Jr. *Formal Education in an American Indian Community*. Kalamazoo: The Society for the Study of Social Problems, 1964.

Werner, Walter et al. *Whose Culture? Whose Heritage?* Vancouver: University of British Columbia Centre for Curriculum and Instruction, 1977.

Whitehead, Margaret. *The Cariboo Mission: A History of the Oblates*. Victoria: Sono Nis Press, 1981.

Whyte, William Foote. *Street Corner Society: The Social Structure of an Italian Slum*. Chicago: University of Chicago Press, 1955.

Willis, Paul. *Learning to Labour: How Working Class Kids Get Working Class Jobs*. New York: Columbia University Press, 1977.

Wilson, J.D. " 'No Blanket Worn in School': The Education of Indians in Nineteenth Century Ontario." In Barman et al. *Indian Education in Canada, Volume 1, The Legacy*. Vancouver: University of British Columbia Press, 1986.

Wilson, J. Donald and D.C. Jones, eds. *Schooling and Society in Twentieth Century British Columbia*. Calgary: Detselig Enterprises Ltd, 1980.

Witvliet, Theo. *A Place in the Sun Liberation: Theology in the Third World*. London: SCM Press, 1985.

Woolcott, Harry F. *A Kwakiutl Village and School*. Toronto: Holt, Rinehart and Winston, 1967.

INDEX

CELIA HAIG-BROWN grew up on Vancouver Island. She has a B.A. in Zoology and English, a teaching certificate, an M.A. in Education, and a Ph.D. in Social and Educational Studies from the University of British Columbia. She taught for five years in Kamloops secondary schools and was Co-ordinator for the Native Indian Teacher Education Program there for most of a decade until 1986. Currently, she teaches at Simon Fraser University in Burnaby, B.C. *Resistance and Renewal* won the Roderick Haig-Brown Regional Prize of the B.C. Book Prizes in 1989.